*The Aquinas
Prescription*

Gerald Vann, O.P.

The Aquinas Prescription

St. Thomas's Path to a
Discerning Heart,
a Sane Society,
and a Holy Church

SOPHIA INSTITUTE PRESS®
Manchester, New Hampshire

Sophia Institute Press®
Box 5284, Manchester, NH 03108
1-800-888-9344
www.sophiainstitute.com

Nihil obstat: Ernest Messenger, Ph.D., Censor Deputatus
Imprimatur: E. Morrogh Bernard, Vicar Generalis
Westminster, September 25, 1940

Library of Congress Cataloging-in-Publication Data

Vann, Gerald, 1906-1963.
    The Aquinas prescription : St. Thomas's path to a discerning heart, a sane society, and a holy church / Gerald Vann.
        p. cm.
    Rev. ed. of: Saint Thomas Aquinas. 1940.
    Includes bibliographical references.
    ISBN 1-928832-09-1 (pbk. : alk. paper)
    1. Thomas, Aquinas, Saint, 1225?-1274. I. Vann, Gerald, 1906-1963. Saint Thomas Aquinas. II. Title.

B765.T54 V3 2000
189′.dc21   00-024785

00 01 02 03 04 05   9 8 7 6 5 4 3 2 1

Contents

Editor's note: The biblical quotations in the following pages are based on the Douay-Rheims edition of the Old and New Testaments. Where applicable, quotations have been cross-referenced with the differing names and numeration in the Revised Standard Version, using the following symbol: (RSV =).

Preface

The following pages were written in the hope of interesting, not primarily the Catholic student of St. Thomas, but the non-Catholic reader who finds himself attracted by the breadth and depth of his wisdom, yet repelled by what he conceives as too exclusively rational an approach to reality, an approach that, as he sees it, diminishes the immensity of truth. I feel that this conception of Thomism is understandable indeed, but tragically false; and I have therefore tried to show both how it may arise and — by setting it against what seems to me a truer and more complete view — why it is false.

An important preliminary caveat must be made to avoid possible misunderstanding. Since this essay was written, E. I. Watkin has published his valuable study *The Catholic Centre*, in which he argues that Catholic doctrine "brings together and reconciles in its comprehensive and balanced truth the partial truths taught by other religions, rejecting only their denials, their exclusions, and their partialities," but that, since Catholicism, "as actually practiced and understood," is practiced and understood by "human beings, with their human limitations, it is never in the concrete a perfect *via media*, or exactly central."[1] That distinction and that double thesis seem to me to be of the profoundest importance, today perhaps more than ever.

What follows, then, is a reaffirmation of faith in the completeness of the center, and nothing could be further from that conviction than to wish to imply any flaw in the divinity of the Church, the continuance of the Christ-life on earth.

On the other hand, it is, unhappily, equally true that the human beings who are members of the Church are always falling short of and betraying its perfection — as we know only too well the moment we look into our own souls. There is nothing lacking to the divinity of the Church; there is much that is lacking in our humanity, and it is our plain duty to recognize and acknowledge the fact.

[1] Edward Ingram Watkin, *The Catholic Centre* (London: Sheed and Ward, 1939), 1-2.

The distinction between reason and intuition will be found to recur frequently in the following pages. I should explain that I am using the term *intuition*, not in the strict scholastic sense of nonconceptual knowledge, but in the more general and colloquial sense of knowledge that is independent of, and distinguished from, discursive reasoning.

"Loss of selfhood in God," and other similar phrases, are, of course, to be understood here, not as implying a pantheist absorption in the deity or loss of personal identity, but simply as expressing the fact that we become truly ourselves, we "find our lives," only through complete surrender of the will to God, and through union with Him, in Christian love and humility, so that we see and love all things in Him and will what He wills, making our discovery of unity in His immensity and finding our freedom in His service.

Being no historian, I have borrowed freely, for my background, from the historians — in particular from Étienne Gilson and Christopher Dawson. Discussion with Anglican theologian friends has enabled me to see far more clearly than I could otherwise have done into some of the issues involved.

Finally, but above all, it is to my friend Fr. Mark Brocklehurst, O.P., that I chiefly owe my understanding of the central thesis of the book, and my realization of its importance. Failures, either of understanding or of presentation, are attributable to me; any claim that may be made to achievement must be made, to say the least, only in association with him.

Gerald Vann
March 9, 1940

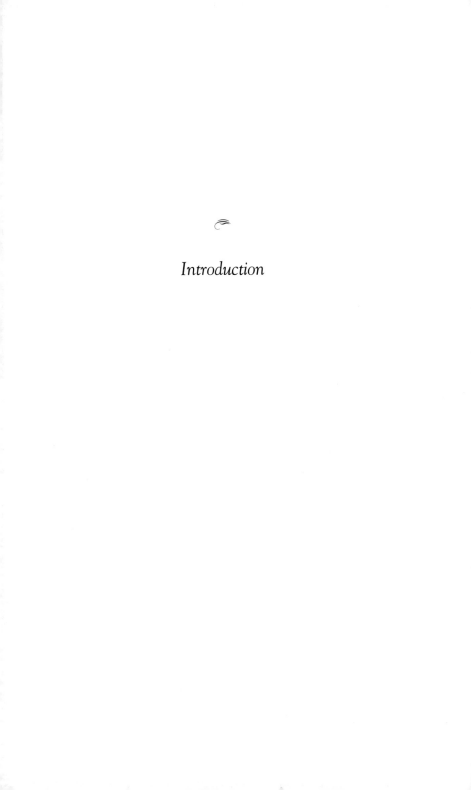

Introduction

Europe has long since passed the stage at which an accusation of intellectual decadence could be met with a stare of shocked and incredulous surprise. The intoxication of nineteenth-century optimism, the conviction that the human race was marching triumphantly forward to a golden age, marching with Europe proudly in the van and altruistically penetrating the outer regions of darkness in order to bring them the light of day at last — all this is over. We begin to see ourselves as others see us, or at least to recognize our real condition.

We are in the position of men having at their disposal numberless alternative means of swift and commodious transport but no place to go. There are, it is true, masses of people who are ready and eager to be dogmatic as to what our destination ought to be. There are those who have an all-too-definite place to go, in the most literal and material sense: a place situated within the confines of their neighbors' territories. There are large numbers of people who "are marching, with banners flying, into the future, 'without God and without hope in the world.' They have pinned their faith to science, unaware that science cannot save the world, since it must serve and cannot lead."[2] There are others who hold to an older and, if we view the history of the world as a whole, more normal view, but who are powerless to put their ideas into effect. Between these conflicting views and theories, the West is tossed and bears every appearance of drifting pilotless to destruction.

It is something to recognize that there is something wrong. But obviously it is not enough. A merely negative attitude will get us nowhere. The West is decadent — and the deepest decadence is to be found in those circles that loudly proclaim the youthful vigor and purity of their way of life; but it will hardly recover its lost vitality unless it can rightly diagnose the causes of its disease. One of the best ways of doing so, perhaps, is to withdraw ourselves from the confusion of angry and conflicting voices and to look at ourselves, collectively, as others see us.

[2] John Macmurray, *The Structure of Religious Experience* (London: Faber and Faber Limited, 1936), 10.

"And she had a sister called Mary, who, sitting also at the Lord's feet, heard His word. But Martha was busy about much serving. Who stood and said, 'Lord, hast Thou no care that my sister hath left me alone to serve? Speak to her, therefore, that she help me.' And the Lord answering, said to her, 'Martha, thou art careful and art troubled about many things. But one thing is necessary. Mary hath chosen the better part, which shall not be taken away from her.' "[3]

Christian tradition has seen in Martha and Mary the symbols of the active and the contemplative life and, in the words of Christ, the right scale of values in regard to them. But that scale of values is not confined to Christianity. On the contrary, it is common to all the great civilizations of the world with the exception of the modern West.

What, ultimately, is the radical difference of outlook that cuts us off from the East, from antiquity as a whole? We shall find its deepest roots revealed to us in the story of Mary of Bethany.

People of the West are accustomed to despise the East for its inertia, its lack of enterprise, its inattention to

---

[3] Luke 10:39-42.

what they regard as progress, the fact that the centuries have not made its streets any cleaner, its sanitation more efficient. They want it, in a word, to be busy about many things.

But the East is ready with its retort: One thing is necessary — and the Western world, in its hustling concern for material things, its worship of material efficiency, its tendency to think of greatness in terms of captains of industry and grandeur in terms of material aggrandizement, has forgotten the better part. It is shallow, and vulgar, and meretricious; it is busy about many things, but they are the least important things.

Beneath the divergent psychological tendencies of West and East, beneath the confrontation of reason and intuition, action and contemplation, there lies a deeper difference. The active, practical mind tends both to superficiality, that "externalization" of the mind against which the mystics warn us, and also to self-sufficiency and egocentricity, to absorption in the question "What am I going to *do?*"

The intuitive, contemplative mind, on the other hand, tends rather to despise the just claims of the superficial in its absorption in the deeper things. It tends also to forgetfulness of self; it tends to find its happiness precisely in self-loss, to make its chief question "What is *he* going to *be?*"

Consequently, in terms of religion, it is the active mind that tends to moralism, to reduce the relationship of creature to Creator simply to the accurate drawing up and observance of rules of conduct. The contemplative mind puts before these things the quest for that self-loss which is on an entirely different plane from ethical unselfishness, and in which indeed it sees the ultimate reason for ethical unselfishness.

It follows that, as each of these types of mind has its own specific richness and its own dangers, the soundest, fullest, and deepest life is to be found in the fusion of both. There are individuals who achieve this fusion in their own personality; for others it is found in the fusion of two personalities in one, the cleaving of two in one flesh,[4] which love effects. And as either in isolation is normally likely to lack balance and completeness, so East and West in isolation are incomplete and need one another, complement one another.

[4] Cf. Gen. 2:24; Matt. 19:5.

It has to be noted at once — and the whole of the study of St. Thomas that follows will necessarily underline the fact — that the Christian view of the story of Bethany is not that Martha is to be condemned and Mary extolled, but only that one way of life, one element in life, is ultimately of more importance than the other. "Martha did not choose ill, but Mary chose better,"[5] says St. Augustine: And in the last resort, action that is the overflow of contemplation is better than contemplation alone. "Just as it is greater to illumine than merely to shine, so it is greater to pass on to others the fruit of contemplation than merely to contemplate."[6]

It remains true that East and West have developed in isolation; and if we are to compare ourselves with the East, we cannot say that it is we who have chosen the better part. It is not we who are normal. Dr. Ananda Coomaraswamy speaks of "the universal metaphysical tradition that has been the essential foundation of every past culture, and which represents the indispensable basis for any civilization deserving to be so called." He

[5] St. Augustine (354-430; Bishop of Hippo), Sermon 103.
[6] St. Thomas Aquinas, *Summa Theologica*, II-II, Q. 188, art. 6.

continues, "Europe has diverged from this path ever further and further since the thirteenth century; only since that time have Europe and Asia been truly divided in spirit. The true contrast is, then, not so much between Europe and Asia as such, as between medieval Europe and Asia on the one hand, and the modern world on the other."[7]

Christian Revelation, emphasizing as it does that the thing of ultimate importance, the pearl of great price for which all else must be sold,[8] is the finding of God in the loss of selfhood, at the same time teaches that the descent of the Absolute into the world of the relative, the coming of God to redeem the world, sets upon man the duty of working in that world, of building in it the city of God. There is, in other words, a synthesis between action and contemplation.

This synthesis was not in fact achieved, at least completely, except in St. Thomas. The problem of the rival claims of this world and the next, of science and wisdom,

---

[7] René Guénon, "Sacred and Profane Science," trans. Ananda K. Coomaraswamy, *The Visva-Bharati Quarterly* (November 1935): 11.

[8] Cf. Matt. 13:45-46.

of reason and revelation, was precisely the problem that vexed the minds of St. Thomas's predecessors from St. Anselm[9] onward; and the problem was not solved, or was solved in a way that could only lead to disintegration.

In point of fact, it was the fate of the Western world to find itself given over precisely to the policy of disintegration. St. Thomas failed to convince his successors, and instead of the fusion, the synthesis, that would have carried Europe forward, integrating its scientific discoveries, its humanist preoccupations, its political and economic evolution, into an organic whole, there came simply a series of more and more devastating disruptions and dislocations, ending with the loss even of the knowledge that synthesis is necessary, and so, with the chaos in which we find ourselves today.

St. Thomas, who was philosopher (in the strict sense: holding to the validity of autonomous reason and exercising that reason in the search for truth, holding that even God's omnipotence could not compass the contradictory) as well as theologian, solved the problems of action and contemplation, of reason and revelation, of worldliness

[9] St. Anselm (c. 1033-1109), Archbishop of Canterbury.

and otherworldliness. But it was not Thomism that was destined to hold sway in the immediately succeeding centuries. The synthesis was broken up. The gap between theologians and philosophers widened, the former becoming more and more distrustful of the latter, the competence of reason with regard to ultimates becoming more and more rigorously curbed.

Scotus,[10] narrowing the field considerably, is followed by Ockham,[11] who denies that reason can prove anything whatsoever about God. Metaphysics degenerates into the futile discussion of logical and even grammatical problems for their own sake. The vital problems of the thirteenth century are replaced by the logomachies that "Sir Thomas More compared to the process of milking a he-goat into a sieve."[12]

Some, anticipating in this a contemporary program, "pinned their faith to science, unaware that science cannot save the world, since it must serve and cannot lead."

[10] Johannes Duns Scotus (c. 1265-1308), medieval Franciscan philosopher.

[11] William of Ockham (c. 1285-1347), philosopher, theologian, and polemicist.

[12] Cf. Christopher Dawson, *Medieval Religion* (New York: Sheed and Ward, 1934), 93.

Some, like Nicolas d'Autrecourt, who bears a startling resemblance to David Hume,[13] relapsed into a despairing subjectivism. Some, determined at any rate to hold fast to the "one thing necessary," held philosophy and science a vanity and concerned themselves exclusively with the devout life.

On the other hand, the humanists of the Renaissance, horrified at the linguistic barbarities of the Scholastics, scornful of the unreality and sterility of their discussions, simply passed them by.

The Scholastics, for their part, made little or no attempt to address themselves to the new state of affairs, to integrate the progress of science or the interests of humanism into their philosophy, or even to defend that philosophy. Luther,[14] trained in Scholastic theology but hating it, was ruder about the reason, about philosophy, than even Peter Damian[15] had been.

The first stage of the disruption was complete.

[13] David Hume (1711-1776), Scottish philosopher and historian.

[14] Martin Luther (1483-1546), leader of the Protestant Reformation in Germany.

[15] St. Peter Damian (1007-1072), reformer and Bishop of Ostia.

"After the reformers and the humanists, the men of the sixteenth century found themselves confronted with a theology without philosophy: the positive or modern theology of Fr. de Vitoria and of M. Cane; and a philosophy without theology: the purely rational speculation of R. Descartes and of Francis Bacon." And this state of affairs was simply the natural development of what had gone before: "the so-called modern conditions of both theology and philosophy were the practically unavoidable upshot of at least two centuries of medieval speculation. For indeed, between the harmony of faith and reason as achieved by Thomas Aquinas and their radical divorce, there was no room left for an intermediate position."[16]

What we need now — and, to misquote Augustine, it is our business not to mourn over the past, but to take heed for the future — is integration. We have at our disposal all the material for building a sane and happy world, if only we can rediscover the one thing necessary, without which we are bound to drift, and to drift to destruction. Our problem is still, as it always has been and always will be, ultimately the problem of religion, of theology.

[16] Étienne Gilson, *Reason and Revelation in the Middle Ages* (New York: Charles Scribner's Sons, 1938), 94.

The Aquinas Prescription

Having rediscovered our religion, we may rediscover our culture, for in our religion we shall be able to integrate our experience, and our mastery, of the relative.

To do that adequately, we need philosophy, and so we shall return to the problem of the Middle Ages, the relation between reason and faith. And in searching for the true philosophy, we shall, if the experience of past centuries means anything to us, avoid from the very beginning the provincial, the partial.

It is to be expected that a philosopher will bear, in nonessentials, the mark of his age and race; he will speak in the idiom of East or West, of this century or of that. But metaphysics itself, if it is metaphysics at all, is above time and temporal differentiations; the absolute does not suffer change. We cannot then say of a metaphysic that it was valid for this century but cannot be valid for that: it is either true or false, now and forever. We shall look, therefore, for a philosophy that is valid both for East and for West — which synthesizes what is true in the thought of East and West, and so provides a complete answer to the ultimate problems.

It is precisely because of its obvious completeness, the immense sweep of its synthesis, that many are turning now for guidance to the thought of St. Thomas — turning, and not turning back; for while no one in his senses would adopt the scraps of physical science to be found in St. Thomas (and such an adoption would indeed be a turning back), there is, as St. Thomas himself is at pains to point out, no necessary connection between this physical science and the metaphysic that it is used occasionally to illustrate. To turn to a metaphysic is not to turn back, for the simple reason that, as has just been said, a metaphysic is not in time at all.

No doubt it sounds fantastic to say that in all the centuries of the world's history, among all the geniuses of East and West, there is one man in whom the truth, the complete truth, is to be found. But it has to be noted in the first place that, since it is a metaphysic that is in question, to say this is not to suggest that, with St. Thomas, everything has been said and there is nothing further to be done. On the contrary, the Thomist world view is not an end but a beginning: it means not that there is no further need of thought, but that thought can be begun without fear of sterility.

In the second place, the claim seems far less fantastic if St. Thomas's work is viewed precisely in the perspective of the history of the West. A man's thought is to a great extent conditioned by the thought of those who have preceded him, in the sense that, through them, he finds the material for his own investigation. It is the fact that St. Thomas lived at a time when the different outlooks and heritages of East and West were present together; when all the materials were to hand for the full and complete human synthesis — indeed, and pre-eminently, for the theandric synthesis, the synthesis of human thought, East and West, with divine; and it is the fact also that, since that time, the same opportunity, despite the interpenetration of East and West in later ages, has not occurred again. It is again the fact, as will be seen later, that St. Thomas was, by birth, upbringing, environment, and temperament, fitted to be the mouthpiece for universal, not for provincial, truth. And finally it is the fact that his theological-philosophical synthesis covers the whole realm of reality, from the bare possibility of being to the inner nature of the Godhead, who is Being itself.

There is here, beyond all shadow of doubt, the one thing necessary; there is also the affirmation, in deed as in word, that "it is better to illumine than merely to shine"; there is action, humanism, the world, as well as contemplation, self-loss, God. But above all there is the synthesis without which these things are the source of endless perplexities and perhaps of chaos: there is the "celestial hierarchy" in which alone is fully revealed the *splendor ordinis*, the beauty of truth.

*The Aquinas
Prescription*

Chapter One

*His contemplation
bore fruit in action*

St. Thomas was born at Roccasecca, the family castle near Naples, probably in 1225. He was the youngest son of Landulf, Count of Aquino, and Theodora, Countess of Teano in her own right. We are primarily concerned in this chapter with the way in which heredity, environment, temperament, and character fitted Thomas for the work of synthesis He was to achieve, so it is important to notice at the very beginning how, in his parents, two very different racial currents met. Landulf was of the South: of the Lombard nobility, and nephew, through his mother, of Barbarossa.[17] Theodora was of the North, coming from a line of Norman nobles.

Modern psychology has made one thing at least abundantly clear: it is extraordinarily difficult to be entirely objective in one's thought, to refuse to be influenced by

[17] Frederick I (c. 1123-1190), King of Germany and Holy Roman Emperor.

the rational assumptions and the nonrational prejudices of one's race and time. Too much of our conscious thinking is predetermined by our unconscious; our conclusions tend to be provincial because we are provincial in our approach to our premises.

The dice were loaded in St. Thomas's favor from the very beginning, because he was neither of Northern nor of Southern blood, but of both; and to this may be added the fact that he came of a class that, at any rate, was not likely to be small-minded, in touch as it was with the affairs of empire and papacy — Thomas's grandfather had been Lieutenant-General of the Empire — while it seems to have been in close contact with that first full flowering of Italian lyric poetry, due largely to the influence of the Provençal troubadours, which had its center in the Sicilian court.

For, indeed, one of the most treasured products of this early Sicilian school is the *Lamento* of Rinaldo d'Aquino, St. Thomas's brother. It is the lament of a girl for her lover who has "taken the Cross" and is bound for the *terra d'oltra mare*, the land across the seas. The colorful ships riding at anchor in the harbor, the clash of Christian and Saracen, the cult of chivalry and chivalrous love, the rich civilization of this Southern kingdom, with its mixture of Arab and Greek and Christian learning; behind that, the strife between papacy and empire; the great personalities, Frederick and Innocent; the Franciscan spirit on the one hand and the Order of St. Dominic[18] and the University of Naples on the other — the whole brilliant scene suggested by Rinaldo and his canzone has to be recalled if the personality of Thomas is to be seen in its right setting. For if he was very early to change the world in which his family moved for another very different one, and then, while still only a youth, exchange that for a third, different again, still the world in which we are born leaves its impress upon us, and the atmosphere of an epoch will be felt in the academic life as well as in the life of courts and cities.

At the age of five, Thomas went to the Abbey school of the Benedictines of Monte Cassino. He imbibed more than the learning and culture that the monks had preserved and fostered through the Dark Ages. One question, his biographers tell us, filled his mind: What is God?

The culture of the Benedictines is a theocentric humanism: the liberal arts, not in isolation, not suspended

[18] That is, the Order of Friars Preachers, or the Dominicans, founded by St. Dominic (1170-1221).

in a vacuum, but ordered toward God. The One, here as elsewhere, is the key to the manifold. Thomas already wanted that key. He seems to have made up his mind very early as to what he should be, and there was no doubt that it was his mind and nobody else's.

His family was deeply involved in the struggle between Pope and Emperor. His brothers had joined the Emperor's forces, and those forces had besieged Monte Cassino. It would be an excellent way of making peace with the monks, and at the same time of repairing the family fortunes, if Thomas were to become Abbot. Thomas refused. He wanted to become a Dominican. It was rather as though a Victorian maiden of gentle birth had announced her intention of becoming an actress.

When he was fifteen or sixteen, he had been sent to Naples — the abbey having been again besieged by the imperial forces — to finish his arts course there. The Dominicans, established as an order in 1216, had been in Naples since 1231. They were something quite new in the history of the Church — an entirely new type of religious order. The old idea had been the attainment of sanctity through prayer, study, and manual labor. St. Dominic had a different end in view, and his choice of means was therefore different also. To give to others the fruit of one's contemplation: that was the program. And since the needs that the order was designed to meet were the intellectual needs of the time, there was included in the idea of contemplation the study of current ideas and current problems.

St. Thomas proposed a threefold intellectual life then: contemplation in the strict sense of prayer, mysticism; rational investigation of the things of God, theology, philosophy; and rational investigation of the problems agitating the contemporary world, so as, if possible, to find the right answer to them in the light of eternal truth.

Such an intellectual apostolate demands a great breadth of mind and sympathy, a great vitality, and the ability — to be acquired, it would seem, only through much mental discipline and a complete devotion to truth — never to grow intellectually old and set, never to entrench oneself behind intellectual battlements, those vested interests of the mind which make it opaque, intractable, or uncomprehending when confronted with new ideas, new problems, or new points of view. Not only the superficial fashion of thought, but the sincere approach to the deepest problems of the mind, vary from generation to generation; they are in continuous process of evolution and change. And to attempt to convince one generation with the language and from the standpoint of another is likely to be worse than useless. Hence the need to be always in intimate contact with the thought of the time; to be "ever old and ever new"[19] like the truth itself.

A metaphysic is a thing that is either true or not true; it cannot be dated. A metaphysic that is essentially of the thirteenth century, or the eighteenth or twentieth century, is not a metaphysic at all. But the way in which a metaphysic is presented, the language in which it is expressed, the subordinate problems with which it deals — these things change, and must change, with the general evolution of thought. As it is extraordinarily difficult for an individual to avoid becoming set in a rigid mental formula, immovable both in his way of thinking and in what he holds (by prejudice and convention as well as by conviction), so it is extraordinarily difficult for a society to avoid living in its own past, remaining merely materially faithful to the surface methods and manners of that past, becoming the historian instead of the creator of its life.

[19] St. Augustine, *Confessions*, Bk. 10, ch. 27.

Dominic was determined that the fruit of his followers' contemplation should not fail to do good for lack of contact with the thought of their time. He sent them off to the universities. At Naples, Thomas found them and begged to be admitted among them. When news came that he had actually become a Dominican, Theodora sent word to his brothers, who were with Frederick's troops, that they must bring him home — by force, if necessary. Thomas was expecting trouble. His family had induced the Pope to offer him the abbacy of Monte Cassino with the right to wear the Dominican habit, and then, when that failed, the archbishopric of Naples. Thomas remained firm.

The Master General of the order, John the Teuton, decided to take Thomas with him to Paris. They were intercepted on the way, and Thomas, after a struggle, was carried off to the fortress of Monte San Giovanni near Roccasecca. He was kept a prisoner for more than a year. His sisters tried to argue him out of his obstinacy, and, as a result, one of them became a Benedictine nun. His brothers adopted a more forthright method of distracting him from his purpose and introduced a girl into his prison; Thomas refused to be beguiled. Finally, he either escaped or was released by his family and rejoined his brethren.

They sent him to study at Paris under Albert of Böllstadt,[20] who, even in his own lifetime, was called "the Great." Albert had neither the profound analytic genius nor the ruthlessly critical approach that complemented the synthetic power of Thomas, but he was a man of immense learning, breadth of interest, and scientific curiosity. His literary output was vast and ranged from theology to botany. He was popularly supposed to be a magician; he was, in fact, a clever scientist.

In philosophy, he set out to make Aristotle intelligible to the Latins, convinced that the policy of wholesale uncritical opposition adopted by so many of his contemporaries was radically unchristian. He was determined, in fact, to be faithful to the spirit of Dominic and to concern himself with the intellectual problems of his time. Naturally he aroused a good deal of fierce opposition; and because it was obscurantist opposition, the opposition of the vested interests, it made him angry, so that he wrote with scorn of "certain people who know nothing, but

[20] St. Albert the Great, or Albertus Magnus (c. 1200-1280), medieval theologian, philosopher, and scientist.

yet try to oppose the pursuit of philosophy . . . like stupid animals, blaspheming against things they cannot understand."

His endless energy proves his intellectual vitality; he was mystic as well as scientist and philosopher. He was Ulrich of Strasburg's master. And his interest in learning of every sort was founded on the conviction that the Christian Faith does not oppose or fight shy of knowledge, however new or startling, but, on the contrary, seeks to assimilate it.

When Albert went to Cologne in 1248, Thomas went with him and there finished his studies. He returned four years later, to join the lecturing staff at the convent of Saint-Jacques. He soon became famous. To meet the intellectual needs of his time, to tackle the problems of his time, to talk the idiom of his time — this was what he set out to do. And his contemporaries and biographers emphasize how well he succeeded. There was no question here of browsing gently and academically over bygone problems and their solutions. "He brought up new questions," says Tocco,[21] "inaugurated a new and valuable

[21] William of Tocco, pupil and biographer of St. Thomas.

method of research and demonstration, developed new arguments. Those who heard him thus teaching new things, solving problems and difficulties in a new way, could not but think that God had illumined him with rays of a new light."

In 1256, although he had not reached the statutory age, Thomas was made Master in theology. He is said to have been distressed in mind at the responsibility this imposed upon him. In our present-day world, adrift from the "universal metaphysical tradition," and ruled not by theology but by politicians and captains of finance, this is no doubt hard to understand. But in the Middle Ages, not only in theory but to a great extent also in practice, the hierarchy was upheld. It was not for the theologian to judge of political matters in the light of political theory, or of economics in the light of economic theory; but it was his office to expound the ultimate principles of life, in accordance with which the everyday affairs of life were ultimately to be governed. For the whole of life, ultimately, is to be lived as preparatory to life eternal.

But how shall one man instruct another in eternal truth? Later on, in the *Summa Theologica*, he was to discuss the question formally: Can one man teach another?

And having examined the answer given by Averroës[22] on the one hand and the Platonists on the other, he was to give his own reply: that, as far as human instruction is concerned, the teacher can lead the pupil from the knowledge of things he already possesses to knowledge he lacks, strengthening his *virtus collativa* to see the connection between truth and truth, or helping him to recognize truth by making it more actual, more alive, more concrete.[23] For this, as he notes elsewhere, it is not sufficient to have fullness of knowledge; there must also be an ability to prove one's assertions, and the faculty of exposition.[24]

His inaugural address as Master is still extant. He took as his text the words of a psalm: "Thou waterest the hills from Thy upper rooms: the earth shall be filled with the fruit of Thy works";[25] and the conclusion he wishes to reach is implicit in the words of the opening sentence: "The King and Lord of the heavens has ordained from eternity this law: that the gifts of His

---

[22] Averroës (1126-1198), Arab philosopher and physician.

[23] *Summa Theologica*, I, Q. 117, art. 1.

[24] Ibid., I-II, Q. 111, art. 4.

[25] Ps. 103:13 (RSV = Ps. 104:13).

Providence should reach to the lowest things by way of those that lie between."

"From the heights of the clouds, the showers rain down, and the hills, watered thereby, send down their streams to fertilize the earth. So, from the heights of divine wisdom, the minds of the doctors, symbolized by the hills, are watered, so that, by their ministry, the light of the wisdom of God may reach the minds of their hearers." And he concludes, with that Christian humility which is only the honest recognition of truth, "But although a man cannot, of himself, be capable of such a ministry, yet he can hope to be given the capacity by God: 'Not that we are sufficient to think anything of ourselves, as of ourselves; but our sufficiency is from God.' This, however, he must ask of God, as St. James says: 'If any of you wants wisdom, let him ask of God, who giveth to all men abundantly and upbraideth not. And it shall be given him.' Which may Christ grant to us. Amen."

That humility, complete self-abnegation in the face of truth, is the very basis of St. Thomas's thought. A metaphysic is either universal or it is not a metaphysic. It is not only the particularities of age and race that stand in the way of universality; a man's thought will be colored by his vanity, or his melancholy, by this, that, or the other emotion, unless he can school himself to absolute objectivity. For St. Thomas, truth was the Truth, a Person. The objectivity of the metaphysician is assured by the self-loss of the mystic. The two things are inseparable.

Étienne Gilson speaks of the "impersonal transparency" of the *Summa Theologica*. Like John the Baptist, Thomas was "not the Light, but came to give testimony of the Light,"[26] and no personal factor is allowed to stand in the way, to obscure the light. "Such mastery of expression and of the organization of philosophical ideas cannot be achieved without a full surrender of oneself; the *Summa Theologica*, with its abstract limpidness and impersonal transparency, is the interior life of St. Thomas itself, crystallized under our eyes."[27] Simply to be a *medium* through which the light of truth, of the Truth, might reach the minds of men: that is the whole of Thomas's life. Philosopher, theologian, poet, mystic — all these are one, for all of them are equally lost in the service of the Truth.

[26] John 1:8.

[27] Étienne Gilson, *The Philosophy of St. Thomas Aquinas* (St. Louis: B. Herder Book Company, 1939), 358.

The Aquinas Prescription

It is significant that the opening line of the hymn of St. Thomas usually known as the *Adoro Te* ought probably to read: "*Adoro devote, latens veritas.*"[28] The integrity that will not compromise and the critical spirit that will not defer to any human authority, however exalted, in defiance of objective evidence are reinforced by the mystical apprehension of the fact that truth and God are one.

Thomas's first battle at Paris had been with Guillaume de Saint-Amour, who denied the right of the friars to teach. There were fiercer battles to come. But in 1259, he was sent to Italy, to the papal court at Anagni, where he taught in the *studium curiae;* thence to the *studium generale* in Rome; and then again to the papal court at Viterbo.

During all these years, he was writing, and his output was vast. He used to dictate to three or four secretaries on different subjects at the same time; and yet his works have about them an atmosphere of sober tranquillity that recalls the remark of Cassiodorus about the "vast leisure

---

[28] "Devoutly I adore hidden truth." The prayer actually begins, "*Adoro Te devote, latens Deitas,*" that is, "Devoutly I adore Thee, O hidden God." Cf. Dom A. Wilmart, O.S.B., *Auteurs Spirituels et Textes Dévots du Moyen Age Latin*, 395 ff.

of the cloister." There was no leisure for Thomas. His writings fill thirty-four volumes of double-column print in the Vivès edition.

In 1269, he was suddenly recalled to Paris, and, for four years, he fought incessantly for what he considered the truth, attacked on the one side by the Averroists, on the other by the Augustinians. Not that it is accurate, perhaps, to speak of Thomas himself as fighting; the bitterness was not on his side. Peckham[29] himself, both now and later the most violent of Thomas's opponents, paid tribute to his calmness and sobriety. And indeed, once the personality of St. Thomas has been understood, that sobriety is only to be expected; after all, he himself, personally, had nothing to lose, no vanity to be wounded. He was possessed, as Gilson remarks, "of two intellectual qualities, whose combination in the same mind is rather rare: a perfect intellectual modesty and an almost reckless intellectual audacity. . . . He had intellectual modesty, because he always began by accepting things just as they were. Thomas Aquinas never expected that things would conform themselves to his own definitions of

[29] John Peckham (c. 1225-1292), Archbishop of Canterbury.

them; quite the reverse, what he would call the true knowledge of a thing was the adequate intellectual expression of the thing such as it is in itself. But he had also intellectual audacity, for, after accepting a thing such as it was, he would insist on dealing with it according to its own nature, and he would do it fearlessly, without compromise."[30]

It was this combination of modesty and audacity that lay at the back of his approach to the problem of reason and revelation. He repudiated the idea that truth is dependent on the arbitrary will of God, who might have chosen to make evil good and falsehood true; there are things, self-contradictions, that even God cannot do, because they are in fact the contradiction of the divine nature. "No power, not even that of God, could produce the contrary of what reason apprehends under the direct influence of evidence. . . . St. Thomas recognized this when he referred to the remarkable person Job, who entered into dispute with God. 'This dispute between God and man,' he says, 'may seem inappropriate because of the great distance that separates man from God. But

[30] Gilson, *Reason and Revelation in the Middle Ages*, 71.

we must remember that where truth is concerned, difference of personality is relatively unimportant. To proclaim the truth is to render a person invincible no matter who his adversary may be.' "[31] Thus, the conviction from which St. Thomas started in his treatment of the problem of faith and reason was simply this: that "it was treason to give up an article of Faith in favor of reason, but, in his eyes, it was just as bad to give up reason for the Faith. Indeed, the treason was fundamentally the same in each case, namely, treason against God, the living Truth."[32]

To surrender oneself wholly to the truth, to lose one's selfhood in the light of truth, is to find peace. There are two phrases, used of Thomas by his contemporaries, that have a more than verbal parallelism. He was, they tell us, wonderfully contemplative and wonderfully gentle. His power of concentration was proverbial. He was peculiarly sensitive to physical pain; but when there was question of

---

[31] Pierre Rousselot, S.J., *The Intellectualism of St. Thomas Aquinas* (London: Sheed and Ward, 1935), 71.

[32] A. D. Sertillanges, O.P., *Saint Thomas Aquinas and His Work* (London: Burns, Oates, and Washbourne Ltd., 1933), 38.

blood-letting[33] or a cautery, he had only to concentrate on some problem, to meditate, and he noticed nothing of what was done.

At times, his abstraction could cause embarrassment. "He was painfully bored by meals,"[34] says Père Sertillanges, which is perhaps not surprising in view of the fact that he took them normally in a Dominican priory, but that is certainly not the whole explanation. At home, his friend Reginald of Piperno had to sit next to him to make sure that he neither ate things that would disagree with him, nor starved altogether. But he seems to have been equally abstracted when dining out. Once, at the table of the King of France, at the time when he was dictating the *Summa Theologica*, he embarrassed his Prior by suddenly

---

[33] In those days, a regular institution. The ancient constitutions of the order declared, "The brethren may be leeched four times in the year: first, in the month of September; secondly, after Christmas; thirdly, after Easter; fourthly, after the feast of St. John the Baptist. Apart from these leechings, none shall dare to leech himself, unless the discretion of the Prior shall judge otherwise for some cause in particular cases." At a later date, an amendment was added: "Nowadays the brethren are neither obliged nor accustomed to be leeched, unless the bodily health demands it."

[34] Sertillanges, *Saint Thomas Aquinas and His Work*, 30.

thumping the table and exclaiming that he had seen the answer to the heresy of Manicheism. Royalty was not ruffled, but sent at once for writing materials.

It would be wrong to suppose that his concentration was purely cerebral — very far from it. There is no separation, in his personality, between the philosopher and the man of prayer, between head and heart. He used to say that he had learned far more from his prayer than from all his books. His speculation, lecturing, and dictating always began with prayer, and when his reason found a problem insoluble, he would resort to prayer again.

There is a story that comes from Reginald himself. Thomas was much exercised over a passage in Isaiah. He prayed and fasted and kept vigil, asking for light. Then one night, Reginald heard voices in Thomas's room. Presently the saint called to him; he wished to dictate. He did so; he had elucidated the passage in question. When the dictating was done, Reginald refused to go until he had learned the identity of Thomas's visitors. Thomas, embarrassed, at last told him that the apostles Peter and Paul had been sent to instruct him; he forbade Reginald to speak of it.

Tocco tells us that he was daily in ecstasy. "Is ecstasy the effect of love?" Thomas asks in his treatise on the emotions. And he answers, quoting the words of the Pseudo-Dionysius[35] — that "the divine love produces ecstasy" and that "God Himself suffered ecstasy through love" — that ecstasy means literally "to be placed outside oneself," and this happens both in mind and will. It happens in mind, when a man is "placed outside the knowledge proper to him," whether it be above him, as in the comprehension of things "that surpass sense and reason," or below him, as when "he is overcome by violent passion or madness." It happens in will, when the will is "borne towards something other than itself, so that it goes forth, as it were, from itself."

The first of these ecstasies, then, "is caused by love dispositively, insofar, namely, as love makes the beloved to dwell in the lover's mind: while the more we give our mind to one thing, the less we think of others. The second ecstasy is caused by love directly: by *amicitia*, the love of friendship, simply; by desire, not simply, but in a restricted sense. For by desire, the lover is taken out of himself in a certain sense: for not being satisfied with the good that he has, he seeks to enjoy something outside

---

[35] Pseudo-Dionysius (c. 500), mystical theologian. In these pages, he is also referred to as Pseudo-Denys.

himself; although since he desires this good for himself, he does not go out from himself simply — the movement ends finally within him. But in *amicitia*, a man's love goes out from itself simply; for he wishes good to his friend and does good: caring and providing for him, as it were, for his sake."[36]

As, in the highest forms of human knowledge, mind and heart are joined, so in the search for truth, intellectual curiosity is not enough. In a letter on how to study, St. Thomas wrote, "Don't bother about the source from which truth comes, but commit to memory whatever is truly said." It is an echo of the words of St. Ambrose[37] that he never tired of quoting, "All truth, no matter by whom it is spoken, comes from the Spirit." That quality of heart that can receive truth even from an adversary is the necessary complement of openness of mind.

Thomas, says Père Sertillanges, "formed deep friendships, above all with his loyal and constant companion Reginald, and with his master St. Albert."[38] But even

[36] *Summa Theologica*, I-II, Q. 28, art. 3.
[37] St. Ambrose (c. 339-397), Bishop of Milan.
[38] Sertillanges, *Saint Thomas Aquinas and His Works*, 33.

with Siger de Brabant,[39] the protagonist of Averroism, his relations, according to Grabmann, were cordial. The gentle simplicity, and humor, which caused him to follow without protest when a friar, who did not know who he was and who wanted a companion, hauled him, puffing uncomfortably, through the streets of Bologna, and was rather offensive because Thomas could not walk faster — this aspect of his character is again the effect of the one fundamental orientation of his whole personality to the Truth, who is also the Good. He had learned the lesson thoroughly; it was what gave him his humility and his peace; it also gave him his strength, and the concision and clarity and sureness of touch in his teaching that his contemporaries found so attractive and so compelling.

Peace and power are together in his portrait. "He was tall and dark, inclined to corpulence, and held himself erect. His complexion was the color of wheat, his head big and rather bold. The Viterbo portrait, more or less successfully copied and restored, shows a face impressed with an admirable pacific and unaffected power;

---

[39] Siger de Brabant (c. 1240-c. 1284), Averroist philosopher.

the eyes under the high and candid arches of the eyebrows are serene like the eyes of a child; the features are regular and rather heavy with obesity, but consolidated by the force of the intellect behind; the mouth is sensitive with regular, well-defined curves, a mouth which never told a lie."[40]

The obstinate strength of the early years, when he faced the opposition of his family, remained with him through all the struggles, the violent diatribes and attacks of opponents, in Paris. Siger de Brabant and his school were, of course, against him. The Augustinian theologians were against him. Peckham attacked him violently. Many of his own brethren abandoned him. Étienne Tempier, the Bishop of Paris, wanted to condemn him in 1270 and, having failed then, succeeded later. Albert, who had borne the brunt of the early attacks from the anti-Aristotelians, had always been ready to give as good as he got; Thomas went placidly on his way, and except for one brief passage in the *De Unitate Intellectus* ("On the Unity of the Intellect"), where a note of scorn creeps into his voice at the tactics of his

---

[40] Jacques Maritain, *The Angelic Doctor* (New York: Dial Press, 1931), 39-40.

opponents, susurrating in corners instead of coming out
into the open, his treatises might have been written in
a region where controversy and hostility were unknown.
He was writing for more than his own age.

The wholeness of St. Thomas's approach to truth,
affective as well as rational, was no enemy to his critical, scientific spirit. On the contrary, here as elsewhere
he was an innovator, as Tocco notes. At the papal court,
he had met the Greek scholar William of Moerbeke; and
as Thomas, urged by the popes to write commentaries on
the works of Aristotle, insisted on accurate translations
direct from the Greek, Moerbeke provided them.

His actual method of commenting was new: he abandoned the old method of paraphrase and substituted a critical textual analysis. His attitude toward patristic texts
was similarly "in keeping with a positivistic-historical
mentality unprecedented in the Middle Ages."[41] As with
the texts, so with the authority of the texts: "Thomas recognized . . . that the Fathers of the Church, for all the
reverence due to them, were not inerrant. . . . He rever-
enced authority, but he declined to be intimidated by it."

[41] Victor White, O.P., *Scholasticism*, 22.

And while he had "the deepest respect for the genius, not only of Aristotle, but also of the Arabs . . . an uncritical acceptance of authority in the exclusive sphere of reason was unthinkable to him, and he did not hesitate to expose the falseness of their views and their arguments when they appeared untenable."

Again, "as he refused to allow human authority to intimidate him, so he insisted that dialectical method must be his servant and not his master. The Scholastic method had by this time become unmanageably complicated and rigidly stereotyped. Too often had dialectical argument become an end in itself, employed for the discussion of futile subtleties (concerning which Thomas was unusually scathing) instead of an instrument for the discovery of truth. Here, as often happens, the perfection of technique had defeated its own ends.

"Thomas set about the simplification and rejuvenation of the Scholastic method. He saw its value too clearly to scrap it entirely, but in his hands the recognized forms of syllogistic argument and counter-argument 'did not tend toward dialectical artificiality, but were employed in the interests of a practical methodical doubt.' When it did not serve his purpose, he abandoned the Scholastic method altogether, as in his *Opuscula* and *Contra Gentiles.*' "[42]

He would not have roused the enthusiasm and devotion of the arts schools as he did had he been the dusty academic technician that a first hasty reading of his work may lead one to think him. His interests were bounded by the demands of his work — and if one sets out, as he did, to create a synthesis that shall comprehend and unify the whole domain of human metaphysical thought, one can hardly have much time to spare; but equally, the very universality of that work demands a universality of mind that, while it forgoes the following out of interests in practice, is an assertion in the realm of thought that to man nothing is foreign. So it is that Thomas was "a humanist in the best sense of the word. He failed to see how the study of God's handiwork, in it-self, and as reflected in [profane] writers, could possibly harm our knowledge of God, seeing that this knowledge is in part derived from nature, and is always illuminated and corroborated by nature."[43]

---

[42] Ibid., 23.

[43] Sertillanges, *Saint Thomas Aquinas and His Work*, 65.

"Because of the peculiar character of his work, St. Thomas felt that he could not afford to pass over any author. . . . He was quite impartial. He studied principally the Fathers of the Church, and, in the words of Leo XIII, 'for having venerated them, he inherited the learning of them all.' But he read a good many others as well, especially the philosophers. He was conversant with the historians, lawyers, doctors, orators, poets, grammarians, and geographers of antiquity. He quotes, among others, Ovid, Horace, Caesar, Cicero, Seneca, Terence, Sallust, Livy, Strabo, Valerius Maximus, Galenus, and Hippocrates. . . . He studied the past, not to save himself the trouble of thinking, but to prepare the ground."[44]

And he was not afraid of the beauty of created things, for he held that "the beauty of creatures is nothing else than the likeness of the beauty of God."[45]

His speculative thought and his mysticism were of a piece. Just as, without any danger to the completeness of his union with the supreme Truth, he could give himself to the study and love of created things, for, having found

---

[44] Ibid., 63-64.
[45] *Comment. in Dionys. de Divin. Nomin.*, ch. 2, lect. 5.

the Center, he could turn without fear to the circumference; so his mysticism combines the more personal, more incarnational, piety characteristic of the Western tradition with the impersonal attitude, the concentration on the loss of self in the otherness of God, characteristic of the East. He avoided the dangers of both: on the one hand, the danger of introspection, and of too exclusive a concentration on·the humanity of Christ and the nearness of God — leading respectively to egocentricity, and to sentimentality and the "domestication of God"; on the other hand, the danger of an unchristian acosmism and perhaps of pantheism.

His mysticism, like his theology, is a synthesis of the Dionysian *via negativa*, the path to knowledge of God through the renouncement of all concept, all affirmation, up to the dark vision of "Him who dwells in the shadows," and of the Johannine insistence that the Light has come into the world, that the Word is made flesh in whom is life, the life that is the light of men.[46] In silence and darkness, he adores the hidden Truth, the hidden Divinity; but he does not forget that:

[46] Cf. John 1:9, 14, 4.

Being born, He became our friend.
At supper, He became our food.
Dying, He paid our ransom's price
And reigning, gives eternal good.[47]

Nor does the completeness of his self-oblation to the hidden Truth give a pantheist impersonality to his prayer, for the thought of ultimate union cannot be absent from that joy which, he teaches, is the effect of love.

Thomas achieved what we have a right to expect any philosopher to try to achieve: he expressed in his life the synthesis of his thought.

That is why we can "pass from the philosophy of St. Thomas to his prayer, and from his prayer to his poetry, without any sense of change in the order of ideas. For there is no change. His philosophy is as rich in beauty as his poetry is heavy with thought."[48] And we might add that his prayer combines in itself his poetry and his speculation.

---

[47] St. Thomas Aquinas, *Devoutly I Adore Thee*, ed. and trans. Robert Anderson and Johann Moser (Manchester, New Hampshire: Sophia Institute Press, 1993), 97.

[48] Gilson, *The Philosophy of St. Thomas Aquinas*, 360.

The Aquinas Prescription

O God, in whom is every consolation,
who discern in us nothing that is not your
own gift, grant me, when the term of this life
is reached, the knowledge of the first Truth,
the love of the highest Good.

Give my body, most generous Giver of rewards,
the beauty of clarity, the swiftness of agility,
the aptness of subtility, the strength of impassibility.
Add to these the affluence of riches, the influence
of delights, the confluence of good things, so that I
may rejoice: above, in your consolations; below,
in the pleasantness of the place; within, in the glory
of soul and body; about me, in the delightful
company of angels and of men.

With you, most merciful Father, may my mind
discover the illumination of wisdom; my desires,
the winning of all desirable things; my efforts,
the praise of triumph; there where, with you,
is the escaping of all dangers, the distinction
of mansions, the concord of wills; where reigns
the amenity of spring, the lucidity of summer,
the richness of autumn, the quiet silence of winter.

Grant me, Lord God, life without death and
joy without sorrow; there where reign supreme
freedom, free security, secure tranquillity, joyful
bliss, blissful eternity, eternal beatitude, the vision,
and the praising of Truth, yourself. Amen.

Contemplata aliis tradere:[49] St. Thomas understood, and put into effect, the motto of his order, as he would have said, *formaliter.* Not a life of contemplation with occasional unrelated incursions into the realm of action, nor a life of action with moments of contemplative calm, but a life in which action and contemplation are one, because the action is only intelligible as the expression, the overflow, of contemplation. The action is the contemplation externalized; the beginning and end of both is the service of the Light. There is no question here of a dilemma between gaining the whole world and saving one's own soul: Thomas wanted to gain the whole world, but to gain it for Christ.

Thomas spent his life, and himself, upholding the claims of human reason. But he was not a rationalist. He was an intellectualist. His life is bounded by two

[49] "To pass on to others the fruits of contemplation."

sentences. As a boy, he asked, "What is God?" As a man, he found the answer as far as it is given to the mind in this life to find it, and he cried, "I can do no more, Reginald; I can do no more. Such things have been revealed to me that everything I have written seems to me so much straw."

That was on December 6, 1273. He had been summoned the year before to Italy, to found a *studium generale*. The choice of a place had been left to him, and he had fixed on Naples. The *Summa Theologica* was not finished; he got as far as the treatise on the sacrament of Penance, but there he stopped. "He hung up his harp," says an old chronicler, adapting the psalm.[50] In January 1274, he was called by the Pope to attend the Council of Lyons. He set off with Reginald, but fell ill on the way and, after lying for four days at his niece's castle at Maenza, was taken at his own request to the monastery of Fossanuova to die.

The old English mystics loved to praise the courtesy of Christ. It was at Maenza that occurred what must be one of the most courteous of miracles. Thomas had no

---

[50] Cf. Ps. 136:2 (RSV = Ps. 137:2).

appetite for food; the only thing he felt he could eat was a fresh herring such as he had had in France. There was no possibility of obtaining them here. And then, when they opened the basket of a merchant passing with provisions of sardines, they found it filled with herrings, and not only Thomas, but everyone else in the castle ate of them.

He lay ill for a month in the monastery. With great effort, he had managed to write the short *Responsio ad Bernardum Abbatem* ("Response to the Abbot Bernard") while on his way to Lyons, and now, because the monks begged him, he made a brief commentary on the Song of Songs.

They brought him the Viaticum, and he welcomed it with the words: "Price of my redemption, Viaticum of my pilgrimage, for love of whom I have studied, kept vigil, worked, preached, taught." He died on the seventh of March. He was forty-nine. The Truth he adored was no longer veiled.

"He was the flower and glory of the world," said Albert of his dead friend and pupil. The Paris Faculty of Arts mourned his loss, calling him the Sun of his century. Grabmann remarks, "The relations between humanism and St. Thomas were far more friendly than writers are willing to believe."[51]

The same could not be said with regard to the traditionalist theologians. Three years after Thomas's death, even to the day, March 7, Étienne Tempier issued a condemnation of two hundred, nineteen propositions, some of which coincided with Thomist teaching. In England, Kilwardby, the Archbishop of Canterbury, himself a Dominican, issued similar decrees. The Franciscans forbade the study of St. Thomas to all except outstandingly intelligent lecturers,[52] and even so, only with the animadversions of William de la Mare. Peckham, who succeeded Kilwardby in the see of Canterbury, reinforced his censures in 1284 and 1286 in the more colorful language that seems to have been habitual with him: "Wishing to apply, as far as may be, to this cancerous itch the medicine of our pastoral charge."[53]

On the other hand, the General Chapter of the Dominicans in 1278 officially adopted the teaching of St.

---

[51] M. Grabmann, *La Filosofia della Cultura secondo Tommaso d'Aquino*, 156.

[52] Cf. M. de Wulf, *History of Medieval Philosophy*, Vol. 2, 37.

[53] Cf. Ibid., 42.

Thomas, and the *Correctorium Fratris Thomae* of William de la Mare was answered by more than one *Correctorium Corruptorii* from the order.[54] The opposition had ignored the attitude of the papacy, both during Thomas's lifetime and after; but with his canonization in 1323 by John XXII, who declared roundly, "Thomas alone has illumined the Church more than all the other Doctors together," the campaign against him ended. The Paris censures were withdrawn the following year; those at Oxford seem never to have been officially withdrawn, but were allowed to remain a dead letter. Nicolas Trivet gently remarks that, in his view, the episcopal authorities had acted too hastily.

The end of the thirteenth century saw the rise of a flourishing school of original thinkers, substantially Thomist, in France, Germany, Italy, and England.[55] In the fourteenth and fifteenth centuries, works of Thomas were

---

[54] Among the Dominicans a generation after St. Thomas, William de la Mare's "correctory" of Thomas — which was based on the difference between Thomas, Augustine, and Bonaventure — was known as a "corruption" of the teachings of St. Thomas, and their response to it was known as the "correction of the corruption" (*Correctorium Corruptorii*).

[55] Cf. A. M. Walz, O.P., *Compendium Historiae Ordinis Praedicatorum* (Rome, 1930), 141.

translated into Greek and Hebrew. Great commentators, with Capreolus,[56] *"princeps Thomistarum,"* at their head, defended, elucidated, and carried forward the work of their master. An immense array of papal documents testifies to the continued support and approval of Rome.[57] At the sessions of the Council of Trent, the *Summa Theologica,* alone of all human documents, was set upon the altar with the Bible.

And yet St. Thomas failed to convince the bulk of his successors. It is significant that the Council of Lyons, to which he was summoned at the end of his life, had been called in order to put an end, if possible, to the schism between East and West that for so long had split the Church in two. He was destined not to be there. And after his death, the synthesis that he had created was lost or abandoned; the split widened.

It is since the thirteenth century that Europe has diverged farther and farther from the "universal metaphysical tradition." "Only since that time have Europe and Asia been truly divided in spirit." The fourteenth century is,

---

[56] John Capreolus (c. 1380-1444), Thomist philosopher and theologian.

[57] Cf. Maritain, *St. Thomas Aquinas,* 184 ff.

in the main, a century of disintegration and collapse. There was a conglomeration of schools, but few original thinkers. Scotus died in 1308, and while his followers, with the Thomists, struggled to keep metaphysic alive, the terminist school of Ockham grew rapidly in numbers and importance: Buridan,[58] Peter of Candia,[59] and Gerson[60] in Paris; Adam Wodeham in Oxford; and other universities in their turn adopted the modern way in place of the traditional. At the same time, the influence of terminism produced the futile cult of dialectic for its own sake, the study of "speculative grammar," the rise of that barbarous latinity which later roused the anger of the Renaissance humanists and which provided such excellent material for the *Epistolae Obscurorum Virorum*.[61] The terminist distrust of reason naturally made the synthesis of philosophy and theology impossible. A Latin Neoplatonist school

[58] John Buridan (c. 1300-1358), French philosopher.

[59] Peter of Candia (c. 1339-1410), Pope Alexander V.

[60] Jean le Charlier de Gerson (1363-1429), French Churchman and spiritual writer.

[61] German humanist and classical scholar Johannes Reuchlin's satirical "Letters of the Obscure Men," which showed the opposition of the humanists to the Scholastics.

had little influence.[62] Latin Averroism expanded anew at the beginning of the fourteenth century, with John of Jandun at its head, and with Padua its principal stronghold. Chaucer's "Bisshop Bradwardyn" at Oxford taught a species of determinism. Nicolas d'Autrecourt, by Bradwardine out of Ockham, developed a pessimist subjectivism. It was not surprising that there should be a reaction from rational speculation and in favor of mystical piety.

The Thomist school, for its part, failed to fulfill the promise of its early vitality. There are great names in the fifteenth century: the Dominicans Capreolus and Antonino[63] (the latter doing pioneer work in the application of Thomist principles to the realm of economics and sociology), and Denys the Carthusian;[64] the universities of Cologne and Louvain were Thomist strongholds, despite

---

[62] Interesting, for the general thesis of this book, to note the comment of de Wulf: "The doctrines of emanation, with their obscure images, and tendency towards pantheism, were not calculated to appeal to the neo-Latin and Anglo-Saxon minds" (*History of Medieval Philosophy*, Vol. 2, 132).

[63] St. Antoninus, also called Antonino (1389-1459), Archbishop of Florence.

[64] Denys the Carthusian (1402-1471), theologian and mystic.

the fact that the inaugural address of the former in 1389 was delivered by a nominalist, Gerard (Kykpot) of Calcar.[65]

And later there begins with Thomas de Vio, usually called Cajetan,[66] the long continuous line of commentators and original thinkers who have been real Thomists in that they have not been content merely to expound and defend the words of St. Thomas, but have carried forward and enriched his work. Cajetan himself was not only a first-rank theologian, but also a biblical scholar and critic whose writings prepare the way, four centuries ahead, for the school of Lagrange.[67] His classic commentary on the *Summa Theologica* is paralleled by that of Franciscus Sylvestris of Ferrara on the *Summa Contra Gentiles*.

In the sixteenth century, a group of thinkers in Spain stand out in startling contrast to the stagnation elsewhere: Vitoria, whose writings on international law have had so profound an influence; Báñez, Medina, Soto, and Melchior Cano; rather later, John of St. Thomas, whose elaboration of the mystical theology of the *Summa* is of

[65] Cf. de Wulf, *History of Medieval Philosophy*, Vol. 2, 215.
[66] Cajetan (1469-1534), Dominican theologian.
[67] Marie Joseph Lagrange (1855-1938), biblical scholar.

particular importance and whose two great *Cursus*, of philosophy and theology, are a profound statement of Thomism as a whole.[68]

In the main, however, the history of Thomism during these centuries is a history of failure, and a failure precisely to achieve the Dominican ideal in the way St. Thomas had so fully demonstrated and so clearly illustrated; a failure to meet the intellectual needs of the times. The vitality of the Spanish school did not spread. Thomists were preoccupied with their controversies with the nominalists; preoccupied also too exclusively with the working out of the purely theological implications of this or that particular doctrine, forgetting the main work of synthesis that is the stuff of Thomism. "Had the Thomists left their wranglings with the nominalists and their purely theological preoccupations to lead the new learning and show how its humanist aspirations found within the Thomist system a fulfillment they could never find outside, the history of the neopagan Renaissance and the subsequent Reformation

[68] Spanish Dominican theologians Francisco de Vitoria (c. 1485-1546), Domingo Báñez (1528-1604), Bartolomeo Medina (1527-1580), Dominic Soto (1494-1560), Melchior Cano (1509-1560), and John of St. Thomas (1589-1644).

would have been very different. As it was, Scholasticism, instead of being, as it had been in the Middle Ages, the sum of all cultural and intellectual enterprise, was rapidly becoming an exclusively clerical exercise more and more out of touch with the world around."[69]

With the loss of the theandric ideal of Thomism — the union of all wisdom and all values, human and divine — there went also the loss of that synthesis between the outlook of East and West which makes St. Thomas so much more than the greatest of the Schoolmen or of Western thinkers. Too often, a material fidelity to particular conclusions reached by St. Thomas masks a radical infidelity to the spirit of Thomism and, in consequence, to the general context in which such particular conclusions should be viewed. This was especially the case with the degradation of Thomist morals into legalism; the shifting of the accent from being to doing and, still more, not doing; an absorption in means to the exclusion of end. It was here especially that "even those textbooks which claimed to be *ad mentem sancti Thomae* differed from him."[70]

---

[69] White, *Scholasticism*, 28.

[70] Dr. Pieper, *Über das Christliche Menschenbild*, quoted in "Extracts and Comments," *Blackfriars* (June 1936.)

But in general, the movement was toward a more and more exclusively Western statement of, and approach to, problems, with the result that the possibility of understanding between East and West became progressively more and more remote. "The study of history," wrote Prince Max of Saxony, "reveals that the West has always wanted to influence the East without understanding it. The spirit of the East has been a stranger to it. . . . They [the Orientals] think that we affect ignorance of their difficulties and reproaches against us. We never go outside our own house; we read only our own books; we look at problems only from our own point of view; and then we ask, with an astonishment that appears naive to the Oriental, how it is that these obstinate men refuse the union offered them by Rome with such abundance of compliments and so much good will."[71]

It is worth recalling that the encyclical *Rerum Orientalium*, urging the study of the beliefs and rites of the East for Western students, remarks that these

[71] *Pensées sur la Question de l'Union des Églises*, quoted by Dom Clément Lialine in *De la Méthode Irénique*, 47 (English translation: *Eastern Churches Quarterly* 3, no. 6 ff. (1939). Dom Lialine notes that the situation today is better but far from perfect.

students themselves will derive from such study a more
fertile understanding of Catholic theology and Latin
discipline.[72] It is worth recalling also that Père Congar,
O.P., in his book *Divided Christendom*, writes, "Divided
Christendom can only be once more wrought into one
Church by means of a more completely effective catholicity. . . . How can there ever be reunion if, instead of
appearing to them as something complete in herself, the
Church looks to those Christians outside her like one
sect among others, an 'ism' as limited and exclusive as
any other 'ism'? Reunion will never become for them a
thing to be desired until the Church is seen to be the
catholicity of the whole Christian inheritance, wherein
they will retain their own spiritual treasures intact, enriched and transfigured in the fullness of communion. . . .
Do we really appear as if we lived in a fullness of life? Do
we not all too often display a meager and insipid kind of
Catholicism, not in the least attractive, so that in us the
resplendent catholicity of the Church becomes small and
repellent? Is Christendom divided first in us, while we
live on part only of our inheritance?" And he goes on:

[72] Cf. Ibid.

"But this would be nothing less than a reform in the Church. It would, and why should we be scared of that? The Church is always reforming herself; it is the way she keeps her life." And, in fact, in the present context, "what else is the inward revival of Catholic theology in the sense of a more serious study of the sources, of the Eastern tradition, of a deeper contemplation of the mysteries, and a deliberate detachment from theological limitations due to the counter-Reformation?"[73]

Père Congar's book is itself a landmark in that work of reform; it is also an eloquent tribute to the new vitality of Thomism in the present day. "It was Leo XIII who first called Thomism out of the theological schools to recommence its task of coordinating human knowledge and getting to grips with the multitudinous problems of the modern world in the light of his thought."[74] Within the confines of the Western world, there was, and is, an immense task of synthesis to be performed; on the other hand, Thomism itself demands the recovery of understanding between West and East, without which the greatest

[73] M. J. Congar, *Divided Christendom* (London: Centenary Press, 1939), 271-272.

[74] White, *Scholasticism*, 31.

Christian problem, the reunion of Christendom, cannot
be achieved. To the accomplishment of that double work
St. Thomas showed the way.

But his world rejected his lead. Perhaps it forgot his
work because it forgot too quickly the spirit in which he
worked.

There are two pictures of the "Triumph of St. Thomas."
One, by Benozzo Gozzoli, depicts a vanquished Averroës
crushed under the foot of the saint. It is a very personal
triumph. One wonders whether Thomas approves of it.
The other is by Fra Angelico, himself a Dominican and
a saint. It depicts Averroës sitting peacefully at the feet
of the saint, as his students did in Paris. Thomas was not
the Light, but was to give testimony of the Light.[75] His
triumph is not in the vanquishing of adversaries, but in
the spread of the light. His triumph will come when we
learn from him the primary lesson of his life, as of his
thought, that it is only in the spirit of surrender of selfhood to the Light that we shall find freedom and truth.

But "the Light shineth in darkness, and the darkness
did not comprehend it." The Light "came unto His own,

---

[75] Cf. John 1:8.

and His own received him not."[76] If we are to see the Truth in its entirety, we must be prepared to say, "*Adoro devote*"; and because we are not prepared, we miss the truth.

"A very simple and modest man was putting everything in its place. His name was Thomas Aquinas, and he was saying things so obviously true that, from his time down to our own day, very few people have been sufficiently self-forgetful to accept them.

"There is an ethical problem at the root of our philosophical difficulties; for men are most anxious to find truth, but very reluctant to accept it. We do not like to be cornered by rational evidence, and even when truth is there, in its impersonal and commanding objectivity, our greatest difficulty still remains; it is for me to bow to it in spite of the fact that it is not exclusively mine, for you to accept it though it cannot be exclusively yours. In short, finding out truth is not so hard; what is hard is not to run away from truth once we have found it. When it is not a 'yes but,' our 'yes' is often enough a 'yes, and . . .'; it applies much less to what we have just been told than

[76] John 1:5, 11.

to what we are about to say. The greatest among philosophers are those who do not flinch in the presence
of truth, but welcome it with the simple words: Yes,
Amen."[77]

---

[77] Étienne Gilson, *Unity of Philosophical Experience* (New
York: Charles Scribner's Sons, 1937), 61.

Chapter Two

*He found the unity
of faith and reason*

It is no longer possible to dismiss the Middle Ages *en bloc* as sunk in "barbarism and religion." Modern scholarship has revealed anew not only the extraordinary vitality, but also the extraordinary fascination, of this springtime of Europe's life.

Intellectually, while Greek philosophy ends with Plotinus and his disciple Porphyrius, and philosophy as such scarcely appears again until ten centuries later, the intervening period is far from stagnant or inactive. On the contrary there is, in the early centuries, a vast activity in the realm of theology, which reaches its climax in the work of Augustine: the grandeur of *De Trinitate* ("On the Trinity") and *De Civitate Dei* ("On the City of God") on the one hand; on the other, the *Confessions*, that magical story in magical prose which has never ceased to capture the imagination and haunt the hearts of men.

The Aquinas Prescription

Then, indeed, there is comparative silence for three centuries — silence, but, again, not inactivity. Père Mandonnet has shown, in his *Siger de Brabant,* how these centuries from the barbarian invasions down to the Renaissance are the history of the restoration and absorption of the Graeco-Roman culture, a process that was achieved in three separate stages.

The first was social: there was a new world to be built on the wreckage of the old; and the world that was built was a new unity, a Christendom, finding its unifying principle in the spiritual rather than in the political order, and basing its social structure on the foundations of Roman law.

This primary task achieved, there is leisure for the things of the spirit, and the second stage of reconstruction is that in which the science and philosophy of Greece is reabsorbed — the twelfth and thirteenth centuries.

With the next two centuries, the third stage is reached: the accent is on aesthetics, the assimilation of literary and artistic forms. Until the breakup of humanism, the process of assimilation was equivalently a search for a synthesis, not a substitution. The tragedy is, as we have seen, that what might have been a continuous process of enrichment of a synthesis established on a metaphysical basis became instead a continuous process of impoverishment due primarily to the loss of metaphysics.

But in the eleventh, twelfth, and thirteenth centuries, the accent is on what is being accomplished and to be accomplished; it is a renaissance, with a youthful note that the later Renaissance, more middle-aged, sobered, and self-conscious, will lack.

Paris has "for the first time become the *patria* of the mind, the rival in men's hearts of Rome"; and men "write hopefully home that 'as Cato saith, to know anything is praiseworthy,' and they live in a garret, with one gown for lectures among them, and play at dice with the neighbor's cat for a fourth. The whole brief sweetness of it in the opening sentence of a story told by an unknown Irish scholar: 'In those first days when youth in me was happy and life was swift in doing, and I wandering in the diverse cities of sweet France, for the desire that I had of learning, gave all my might to letters.'

" 'John of Salisbury writes of Paris with the subdued warmth, the steady heat of his affection transfiguring his sober prose. Guido de Bazoches becomes sheerly lyrical: 'Paris, queen among cities, moon among stars, so gracious a valley [as it is to this day from the terraces of Saint-Germain], an island of royal palaces. . . . And on that island hath Philosophy her royal and ancient seat: who alone, with Study her sole comrade, holding the eternal citadel of light and immortality, hath set her victorious foot on the withering flower of the fast-aging world.' "[78]

The "*patria* of the mind": it was for its intellectual leadership and vitality that Paris was the queen of cities.

And if we need emphasis on our present degradations of shallowness and vulgarity, we need only reflect how, in our own day, the emphasis has shifted, so that what we choose to call our great cities are famous primarily for their political importance or their commercial prestige. Our international debates and rivalries are concerned with the political ownership of this or that strip of territory, these oil fields, those mines.

[78] Helen Waddell, *The Wandering Scholars* (New York: Henry Holt and Company, n.d.), 120, 121-122.

He found the unity of faith and reason

The men of the Middle Ages, like the Greeks, were great politicians, no doubt, but their disputes concerned political philosophy, which is important, and they largely left it to kings and their buccaneering hirelings to play chess with their lands.

What would be still more incomprehensible to the medieval mind would be our habit of making commercial considerations the criterion of value and of judging scholarship and even truth itself in the light of its cash returns. The Paris of the early Middle Ages echoes with the cries and clashes of conflicting parties, but they were battling over things that really matter; they were concerned not with means, with the transient, but with ends, with the ultimate things. If the intellectual world to which St. Thomas came and which he so radically changed is to be understood, it is those battles which must first be discussed.

Scholasticism may be said to begin with St. Anselm. St. Augustine had urged the study of rhetoric; and the tradition of the Roman schools had been carried on and preserved through the Dark Ages by the monasteries, with their curriculum of *trivium* and *quadrivium*, which together comprised the seven liberal arts. It was the grammar, rhetoric, and logic of the *trivium* that developed into Scholasticism, and the development was due to the innovation, startling to his contemporaries, of St. Anselm.

His predecessors had been content to repeat the teaching of the Fathers. St. Anselm returned to the spirit of St. Augustine and applied the technique of the schools to the data of Revelation with a view to gaining greater insight into the things of Faith. "I believe in order that I may understand": this was Anselm's watchword, and, to his contemporaries, it savored of the revolutionary. This was partly due to the fact that they thought it idle to expect that anything could be added to the glories of the patristic period. But there was a deeper source of opposition and hostility.

The perennial problem for any society whose basic convictions are otherworldly, the problem of the validity of created things and the interest in created things, had here an immediate application. "Beware lest any man cheat you by philosophy and vain deceit,"[79] St. Paul had said; and it was easy to ignore other parts of his teaching

---

[79] Col. 2:8.

that provide an exegesis of the text and to use it as a peg on which to hang a condemnation of the use of natural reason. There is only one important thing: salvation. So runs the argument; let us, then, despise and neglect the world. There is only one thing necessary to teach us the way to salvation: the Revelation of God; let us, then, despise and forget the paths to natural knowledge.

Tertullian,[80] Tatian,[81] Peter Damian, Bernard of Clairvaux,[82] the Franciscan Spirituals,[83] the author of the *Imitation*[84] — the list is a long one, and its attitude is summed up in the words of Tertullian: "What, indeed, has Athens to do with Jerusalem? What concord is there between the Academy and the Church? What between heretics and Christians? Our instruction comes from the

---

[80] Tertullian (c. 160-c. 225), African Church Father.

[81] Tatian (c. 160), Christian apologist.

[82] St. Bernard of Clairvaux (1090-1153), abbot.

[83] The Spirituals were those Franciscans who desired a strict adherence to the letter of their rule and the spirit of their founder, St. Francis of Assisi, as opposed to a more moderate interpretation.

[84] *The Imitation of Christ*, a spiritual classic by ascetical writer Thomas à Kempis (c. 1380-1471).

porch of Solomon, who had himself taught that the Lord should be sought in simplicity of heart. Away with all attempts to produce a mottled Christianity of stoic, platonic, and dialectic composition! We want no curious disputation after possessing Christ Jesus, no inquisition after enjoying the Gospel. With our Faith we desire no further belief. For this is our palmary Faith, that there is nothing that we ought to believe besides."[85]

It was not, of course, speculative thought merely that the antihumanists fell foul of — did not Peter Damian denounce the study of grammar, begotten of the Devil, the first grammarian, who tried to make polytheists of our first parents by teaching them the forms of *deus* in the plural, saying, "Ye shall be as gods";[86] and did not Alexandre de Ville-Dieu expunge from grammar the "great names of Hector and Achilles and Agamemnon" and exercise "his faculty and the quantitative rules on Melchisedech and Noah and Abimelech"?[87]

---

[85] Tertullian, *On Prescription Against Heretics*, ch. 7, quoted in Gilson, *Reason and Revelation in the Middle Ages*, 10.

[86] Gen. 3:5.

[87] Waddell, *The Wandering Scholars*, xix.

But it is speculation with which we are here concerned; and it was this attitude toward it that St. Anselm
had to meet in the eleventh century as St. Thomas did in
the thirteenth.

St. Anselm's position was substantially that of St. Augustine, who had found that "the safest way to reach
truth is not the one that starts from reason and then goes
on from rational certitude to faith, but, on the contrary,
the way whose starting point is faith and then goes on
from revelation to reason."[88]

Now, as Professor Gilson has pointed out, all those
who follow St. Augustine in this view of things — and,
again, the list is a long one — agree that "unless we believe, we shall not understand; and all of them agree as
to what we should believe, but they do not always agree
as to what it is to understand." Anselm "had not gone
through the ordeal of Augustine's conversion and was
not indebted to Plato, nor to Plotinus, for his discovery
of what intellectual knowledge actually is. To him, as
to all his contemporaries, rational knowledge was logical
knowledge. In his mind, and in the mind of his disciples,

---

[88] Gilson, *Reason and Revelation in the Middle Ages*, 17.

a rational demonstration was a dialectical demonstration made up of faultlessly knitted syllogisms. In short, in Anselm's own times, the standard science was logic. In such circumstances, the same endeavor, to achieve a rational understanding of Christian Faith, was bound to result in a new translation of Christian beliefs into terms of logical demonstration."[89]

The danger of this approach is obvious: there will be a tendency to confuse logic with metaphysics — a tendency to try to prove too much; and "second-rate thinkers will use revelation as a substitute for rational knowledge, not without causing serious damage to both revelation and reason.

"The net result of such mistakes always is, first, to render a truly natural knowledge impossible, and, next, to substitute for faith in the word of God a more or less rational assent to the conclusions of pseudo-demonstrations. Thus confronted with a wisdom of Christians, elaborated by Christians, and for the exclusive benefit of Christians, unbelievers find themselves in a rather awkward position. They do not believe; hence they have nothing

[89] Ibid., 22-25.

to understand. The only way out of such a situation
is for them to pit against theology a purely philosophical wisdom, exclusively based upon the principles
of natural reason and independent of religious revelation."[90] That is exactly what happened in the Middle
Ages.

The age of St. Thomas, and the thought of St.
Thomas, cannot be understood apart from the work of
the Arabian philosophers and theologians. The most violent, and the most far-reaching, controversies of the thirteenth century were those that concerned the doctrine
of Ibn Rushd — Averroës, as the Latins called him.

The Arabs, like the Christians, had been devoting
their energies to the harmonizing of faith and reason —
in their case, of the Koran with the predominantly Aristotelian doctrines of philosophy. Ibn Sina, or Avicenna,
had elaborated a philosophical system; Ghazali, the greatest of the Islamic theologians, finding it irreconcilable
with the teaching of the Koran, attacked it in his *Destruction of the Philosophers*. Averroës replied to this in
the *Destruction of the Destruction* and then proceeded to

[90] Ibid., 32.

deal with the whole problem of philosophy and theology in *The Agreement of Religion and Philosophy*, a book that was to have indirectly an immense influence on the Christian thought of the time of St. Thomas. The thesis of the book is expounded by Professor Gilson in his *Reason and Revelation*.[91]

Averroës divides men into three psychological types: those who, where the exposition of truth is in question, can be persuaded by rhetoric; those who have to be approached through dialectic; and those, finally, who demand necessary demonstrations if they are to be convinced.

The first group is swayed by imagination and emotion. It is for them that revelation has been given and prophets sent. They will not be persuaded to order their lives in accordance with true principles by an appeal to reason; they must be persuaded by religious myths, by the promise of Paradise and the threat of eternal torments.

The second group demands motives of credibility, and it is for them that theology is valuable and necessary,

---

[91] *Reason and Revelation in the Middle Ages*, 40 ff.

since the function of theology is to argue the rational probability of the things of Faith.

The third group demands knowledge. They must have necessary demonstrations of the truth; they will not regard the simple faith of other men as wholly false, but they will distinguish in it the basis of truth from the superstructure of fancy.

Thus, Averroës concludes, all these groups ultimately agree, faith and theology providing the nearest approach possible for the mass of men to the absolute truth of philosophy.

This view of things was difficult enough to sustain in a Moslem world, and Averroës suffered for his convictions. But it was impossible in a Christian civilization such as that of Europe in general and Paris in particular, where theology and philosophy were in the hands of churchmen.

In consequence, there arose the theory of the "two truths." There were men, like Siger de Brabant and Boethius of Dacia, who were sincere Christians, and yet at the same time convinced that Aristotle, as expounded by Averroës, was synonymous with reason, infallible. They had no alternative but to teach an irreconcilable antinomy: this is *true* because it is revealed; that is a *necessary* conclusion from the point of view of reason. In other words, they were compelled to adopt an attitude of blind fideism in theology and skepticism in philosophy. There was not much hope for the future, for the universal metaphysical synthesis, in this unhappy compromise.

At the same time, there was another Averroist group that made little or no attempt to compromise, since it was frankly rationalist. It is indeed of immense importance to recognize the existence of this pure rationalism, to recognize that "the Averroistic tradition forms an uninterrupted chain from the Masters of Arts of Paris and Padua to the Libertins of the seventeenth and eighteenth centuries."[92] For it was precisely this rationalism that was the enemy of the scientific spirit — St. Thomas was at pains to point out that the deification of Aristotle, the belief that Aristotle and reason were synonymous and that therefore neither his philosophy nor his physics could be tampered with, was the suicide of philosophy and of science.

At the same time, the belief in the value of reason, the autonomy of reason in its own sphere, was one of St.

[92] Gilson, *Reason and Revelation in the Middle Ages*, 65.

Thomas's preoccupations, a thing that had to be preserved at all costs if the universal synthesis was to be achieved; and the achievement was made all the more difficult by this association of the service of reason with rejection of faith.

That the Aristotelianism of Averroës was in fact incompatible with Christian truth is sufficiently obvious. Aristotle, in his analysis of intellect in the De Anima ("On the Soul"), had distinguished a passive and an active intellect: knowledge means the actualizing of the intellect as passive, receptive, potential, by the assimilation of the forms or essences of things, and this process requires an active, actualizing power, which the "active intellect" supplies. What precisely Aristotle meant by this analysis has always been matter for debate. Theophrastus considered both the intellect that "makes" and the intellect that "becomes" as together forming the one human intellect. Alexander of Aphrodisias held the active intellect to be one eternal substance, identified with deity. Themistius denies this identification with the deity, but agrees that the active intellect is one for all men.[93]

---

[93] Cf. R. D. Hicks, Aristotle De Anima, lxiv-lxv.

The Aquinas Prescription

The Aristotelianism of the Arabs was deeply impregnated with Neoplatonism, and it is natural to find them inclining to the view that the active intellect is one, common to all men, a stage in the process of cosmic emanation. This was the view of Avicenna; it was also the view of Averroës. But the latter went further.

Averroës limits individual intelligence to the sphere of the corporeal, of imagination, and holds that knowledge is acquired only through union with the common "separated" intellect. He is thus led, since the psychic element in individuals is not immaterial, to deny personal immortality. Similarly, he has no place either for creation or for particular Providence.

But if the Averroism of Averroës was incompatible with Christianity, that of some of his Latin followers was still more so. St. Thomas, suspect because of his devotion to a pagan philosopher who was presented in so antichristian a manner, narrowly escaped condemnation in 1270 at the hands of the Bishop of Paris, Étienne Tempier. In 1277, he did not escape, and the condemnation was officially withdrawn only in 1325. But from the fact that Thomism was included in these censures, it must not be concluded that the bishop was merely an obscurantist reactionary:

there was good reason for the condemnation of the Averroist propositions. "There is no higher life than philosophical life," one of these maintained; another: "Nothing should be believed, save only that which is either self-evident, or can be deduced from self-evident propositions"; again: "Christian Revelation is an obstacle to learning"; "Theology rests upon fables."[94]

The problem of faith and reason is here solved by an expedient as simple as, and complementary to, that of the antihumanists: that of eliminating one of the two terms. If, on the one hand, St. Thomas had to face and combat an uncompromising fideism, on the other, he was compelled equally to fight a forthright rationalism. And it is good to emphasize — for the understanding of his own refusal to compromise with rational certitude, or to do violence to the autonomy of reason in its own sphere — that for him, too, Averroës continued to be "the Commentator" par excellence of Aristotle and a valued ally in many of the problems of philosophy.

The influence of Neoplatonism on the minds of the Arabian philosophers was profound, and it is important

[94] Gilson, *Reason and Revelation in the Middle Ages*, 64.

to remember that the rationalist approach of an Averroës was counterbalanced by the mysticism of an Avicenna or a Ghazali. For these latter, the end of man is the achievement of union with the supreme intelligence by way of mystical exaltation, of the ecstasy of the Neoplatonists. Their view was shared by the Jewish thinker ben-Gabirol, or Avicebron,[95] held in high esteem by the Franciscan school, who taught a form of Plotinianism colored by the thought of Philo the Jew,[96] a syncretism of Hebraic and Neoplatonist elements.

Another Jewish thinker, Moses Maimonides,[97] is of even greater importance. The most balanced, with St. Thomas, of all the medieval thinkers, according to Gilson, Maimonides addressed himself to the problem of reason and revelation, convinced that, truth being necessarily one, there could be no contradiction between them. Predominantly Aristotelian, his thought is nevertheless influenced by Neoplatonism and goes to extremes in its emphasis on the *via negativa*, on agnosticism, in the question of the knowledge that man can have of God.

[95] Salomon ben-Gabirol, or Avicebron (c. 1020-c. 1070).

[96] Philo (c. 20 B.C.-c. 50), Jewish thinker and exegete.

[97] Moses Maimonides (1135-1204).

There is another important factor that must not be forgotten if the picture of the medieval setting is to be complete. It was not only works of patristic theology that were "discovered" in the eleventh and twelfth centuries, but the pagan classics as well. "Latin verse composition had always, of course, been taught. Charlemagne bent his great brows on the young dandies of the palace school who failed to produce tolerable verse, and Hrabanus Maurus came to Alcuin at Tours to study metres. But it is towards the end of the eleventh century that one recognizes the beginning of the craze for verse, which is almost universal in the twelfth, just as in Elizabethan England any man of breeding was expected to know what to do with the music sheet set down before him after dinner."[98]

The importance of the revival of profane learning and poetry can hardly be overemphasized. There was violent opposition, of course. " 'I believe,' said Master Konrad Unckebunck, 'that the Devil is in these poets. They destroy all universities.' "[99] That was later, but, from the first, the humanists found themselves at daggers drawn

[98] Waddell, *The Wandering Scholars*, 101-102.
[99] Ibid., 135.

with the prevalent theology. For the prevalent theology was that of the self-styled Augustinians, "confusing, in their material attachment to the literal interpretation of their master, the formal objects of faith and reason, of metaphysical wisdom and the wisdom of the saints — inclining, in short, to what we should nowadays describe as anti-intellectualism."[100] But if the prevalent attitude was one of reciprocal opposition and dislike, it remains true that the revival "gave a humanistic direction to much Scholastic thought of this period, especially in the schools of Chartres,"[101] and that, in the total mass of material to be unified in the universal synthesis, the love of poetry and letters, the spirit of humanism in general, held a large place.

Before attempting to summarize the diverse and often contradictory trends in this mass of material, we must return for a moment to St. Anselm. There are two points to be mentioned. In the first place, "it would be entirely to misunderstand him (and indeed the whole spirit of the more reputable Scholasticism) to suppose that he was a

[100]Maritain, *The Angelic Doctor*, 118.
[101]White, *Scholasticism*, 12.

mere intellectualist. The way from faith to understanding is for Anselm an affair of the heart and the soul, as well as of the head; ethical and religious, as well as dialectical. He insists repeatedly that intellectual acumen is of itself insufficient. 'It is clear,' he writes, 'that man must concentrate all his powers to the contemplation, understanding, and love of the supreme Good.' "[102]

In the second place — and it is in this that his chief importance lies — he did not "confine the role of reason to 'understanding' particular articles of Faith. It is, above all, for his utilization of rational method for the *systematization* of the truths of Christian doctrine that he is important and original. In applying reason to the data of authority in order to penetrate its meaning, he did no more than revive the practice of Augustine and other Fathers and Doctors of the Church, but by the conscious application of reason to *coordinate* and *synthesize* those data and the deductions to be drawn from them, he opened entirely new ground. Though Anselm himself did not, indeed, undertake any such comprehensive systematization of the whole corpus of Christian doctrine,

[102] Ibid., 9.

he laid the foundations for future work by his synthetic treatment of the central doctrines of Christian belief, in particular of the Trinity, the Incarnation, and the Atonement. By employing methodical dialectic for the attainment of a deeper and more embracing understanding of all aspects of particular dogmas, he was led to see their essential interrelation one with another, and the essentially organic character of the corpus of Christian doctrine. The analogies of supernatural and natural truths became apparent to a degree which had not been appreciated hitherto. In this, more especially, he was the 'Father of Scholasticism.' "[103]

What, then, were the elements that had to be integrated if the synthesis was to be achieved? There was, first of all, of course, the Christian Revelation, viewed, so to say, in abstraction from the varying ways in which its truth was applied to the realm of reason and nature. Second, there were the currents of Jewish thought, as embodied in the Christian religious tradition, and also as expressed in the thought of the Jewish philosophers. Third, there was the influence of Platonism and Neoplatonism,

[103] Ibid., 9-10.

present with many variations in Augustine, Porphyrius, Boethius, the Pseudo-Denys, and Avicenna; fourth, the antirationalist theologism of the Augustinians; fifth, the antireligious rationalism of the Averroists; sixth, Aristotle himself, as presented in the literal translations from the Greek of such men as William of Moerbeke; seventh, the legacies of Roman and Judaeo-Christian law, as yet unsynthesized, and the Roman-legal attitude of mind; eighth, the humanist cult of letters, and the legacy of classical poetry; ninth, the development of a mystical tradition that combined Eastern and Western currents; tenth, the idea of knowledge not primarily as a means to practical achievement, not as an epiphenomenon of life, but as the highest kind of life, in which, however, the intellect could not be viewed in abstraction from the heart, the will; and finally, the recognition of the organic character of Christian truth, and the idea, implicit in it, of a universal synthesis to include the whole universe of being, natural and supernatural, human and divine.

That such a synthesis, built upon these materials, would have to be something very different from a simple grouping together of diverse elements, an eclecticism, needs no stressing. It was a question not simply of unifying the disparate elements of a complete culture, but, first of all, of finding the truth between contradictory theories, of solving the deepest problems that confront the human mind.

Is the one thing necessary to be regarded exclusively, so that there can be no place in the Christian life either for the world in general, or for the light of reason, the profane sciences and philosophy, and culture, in particular? If there is a place for reason, must it be simply as, in Jerome's phrase, the handmaid of theology, in the sense that philosophy can have no point or validity of its own, and that reason, dialectic, must simply serve for the elucidation of what is of faith? If there is a place for philosophy as such, then where is true philosophy to be found: in Plato, in Aristotle, among the Arabs? If we are to uphold the claims of philosophy to be autonomous in its own sphere, the sphere of rational certitude, shall we not become embroiled in contradictions between reason and faith? And if so, how shall we decide between them without betraying the one or the other? If that fullness of life which is the end of man includes both heart and head, which of these should be given the primacy? The questions are endless.

But it is not enough to answer the questions themselves, one by one; that would not be to create a philosophy, still less a universal theological-philosophical synthesis. If we want to know the answer to the riddle of life and of the universe, if we want to achieve wisdom, if we want to be fully alive, we must discover a view of reality as a whole in which the answers to individual problems will find their functional place in the organic unity of the whole.

It was that unity that St. Thomas set out to find.

It may be good to return explicitly to the central theme of the Introduction, and indeed of the whole of this essay. If St. Thomas did in fact succeed in his search for unity and integration, then he succeeded in unifying the characteristic thought, the characteristic outlooks, of East and West. For what needs to be emphasized is this: that the presence of Eastern wisdom in the West was not a question simply of the adoption by the Western type of mind of a number of particular doctrines that in point of fact were taught in the East. It was a question of a spiritual permeation, the adoption of a spiritual attitude, a temper of mind.

Père Théry has made this very plain in a valuable article.[104] "It seems to me inaccurate," he writes, "to speak of

[104]Père Théry, "*Denys au Moyen Age: L'Aube de la 'Nuit Obscure,'* " *Nuit Mystique, Études Carmélitaines* 2 (October 1938): 68-74.

a 'Dionysian current of thought.' A current of thought is canalized within definite limits. Denys, on the other hand, is in part impossible to seize hold upon. It is not through the Celestial Hierarchy and the Ecclesiastical Hierarchy, with their teaching on the angels and their nature and function, that Denys dominates medieval thought; it is by his suggestions that he is the creator of a temper of mind and a state of soul."

What is the essence of those "suggestions" as revealed, for example, in *Mystical Theology*? Simply that "God dwells among the shadows. If we wish to come to Him, it is in the shadows and by the shadows that we must direct our steps. Sensation and ideas, what is given to sense and to intelligence, the very notion of being and non-being, by the fact that they have a limited and determinate content, hide from us the Undefined and Infinite. Our ideas are light; but because they are light, they illumine only a limited field, and God is without limit. . . . The Dionysian ecstasy is intellectual and moral union with the Infinite beyond all finite sensation, all definite concept: 'Renouncing all things, detached from all things, you will rise to the supersubstantial ray of the divine darkness.' "

Now, this Dionysian approach to the knowledge of
God permeated Europe, as Père Théry goes on to show,
in four separate periods: in the ninth century, with
Hilduin,[105] John Scot Erigena[106] and, to some extent,
Hincmar of Rheims,[107] and Paschasius Radbertus;[108] in
the twelfth and thirteenth centuries, with John of Salisbury,[109] John Sarrazin, the Victorines;[110] then again, a
deeper and more extensive penetration into the thought
of the Franciscan theologians, of Albert the Great,
Thomas Aquinas, Ulrich of Strasburg; finally, the mystics, especially the German mystics, of the fourteenth
century. In the course of that process of penetration,
two developments are to be noted.

First, the "Dionysian 'intellectual' ascesis, which
finds its term in ecstasy," comes more and more to be

[105]Hilduin, Abbot of Saint-Denys and biographer of
Dionysius.

[106]John Scot Erigena (c. 810-c. 877), philosopher.

[107]Hincmar (c. 806-882), Archbishop of Rheims.

[108]St. Paschasius Radbertus (c. 790-865), Benedictine
theologian.

[109]John of Salisbury (c. 1115-1180), medieval humanist.

[110]The canons of the former abbey of St. Victor in Paris,
among whom were many famous scholars, mystics, and
poets.

paralleled by a " 'mental' ascesis which finds its term in detachment from self and creatures, and therefore in the total abandonment of self into the hands of the Father who governs us."

Second, there was the reinforcement of the Dionysian spirit by Arabian and Jewish thought in the thirteenth century: "Denys, the Musulman thinkers, Maimonides, fuse together; if their doctrines differ, the state of soul which they inspire is very similar; and their doctrines are fused in Christian mysticism." Thus the German mystics of the fourteenth century base their doctrines on the combined thought of Denys himself, the Victorines, the Arabs, and Maimonides; and through Eckhart, Tauler, Suso,[111] and the author of *The Cloud of Unknowing*,[112] the tradition holds — "God is a light who shines in the darkness" — and so continues to the later exponents of the theology of the "Dark Night."[113]

[111]German mystics Eckhart (c. 1260-1327), Johann Tauler (c. 1300-1361), and Bl. Henry Suso (c. 1295-1366).

[112]An English mystical treatise of the fourteenth century written by an anonymous author.

[113]A time of purification by which God leads the soul to greater holiness, dealt with extensively by Carmelite mystic St. John of the Cross (1542-1591).

It is the presence of this trend in Christian thought that enables Dr. Coomaraswamy, for example, to argue that "the Hindu 'deification' . . . is precisely what is meant when we are commanded, 'Be ye therefore perfect, even as your Father in Heaven is perfect,'[114] and meant by St. Paul when he says that 'Whoever is joined unto the Lord is one spirit.'[115] A fundamental distinction of Hinduism from Christianity is . . . impossible," for it is primarily the presence of this trend of thought that offers such startling parallels. "One who reaches the end of the road and enters into God must leave behind him the whole burden of his deeds, whether good or evil. For these are the basis of 'character,' and nothing characteristic can enter into the uncharacterized Deity, 'whose only idiosyncrasy is being.' There, as Meister Eckhart says, 'Neither vice nor virtue ever entered in,' or, as the Upanisad expresses it, 'Neither vice nor virtue can pass over that Bridge of the Spirit which is the only link between this world and that.' In the words of Damascene, 'He Who Is, is the principle of the names applied to God'; and the Upanisad, 'He Is: by

---

[114]Matt. 5:48.
[115]1 Cor. 6:17.

that alone can He be apprehended.' It is not, then, by works or merit that a man is qualified to attain the perfection of happiness, but only by an absolute knowledge and love of God; an absolute knowledge or love of anything implying, of course, a perfect sameness of knower and known, lover and beloved."[116]

This, it has been argued in preceding pages, is the temper of mind characteristic of East rather than of West. And set over against it, in the wealth of diverse traditions that met in Europe at the time of St. Thomas, are those other trends that are characteristic rather of the West: the spirit of action, such as had gone into the building of the Roman Empire and the creation of a new order from the wreckage of the old — a spirit, moreover, sanctioned by the place given in Christianity to works, and sanctioned ultimately by the fact of the Incarnation of the Word in space-time; the humanist spirit, the love of poetry and art and all created beauty, which, again, could find its justification in the doctrine of Redemption; the

[116] A. K. Coomaraswamy, "The Indian Doctrine of Man's Last End," in *Asia* (May 1937). The Upanisad is a collection of late Vedic metaphysical treatises that deal with man's relation to the universe.

zest for reason and logic and philosophy and the sciences; the elaboration of law — the *jus naturale*, the *jus civile*, the *jus gentium*; in a word, the concern for the finite and particular and fleeting as well as for the Infinite and the Incomprehensible.

Could these two so divergent outlooks be unified? That was, ultimately, the one question that was being asked, and St. Thomas fearlessly and completely answered it.

Chapter Three

He employed reason
in service of Revelation

"Now, of all human pursuits," wrote St. Thomas at the beginning of the *Summa Contra Gentiles*, "that of wisdom is the most perfect, the most sublime, the most profitable, the most delightful. It is the most perfect, since in proportion as a man devotes himself to the pursuit of wisdom, so much does he already share in true happiness: whence the wise man says, 'Blessed is the man that shall continue in wisdom.'[117] It is the most sublime because thereby especially does man approach to a likeness of God, who 'made all things in wisdom';[118] wherefore, since likeness is the cause of love, the pursuit of wisdom especially unites man to God by friendship; hence it is said that wisdom 'is an infinite treasure to men, which they that use become the friends of God.'[119] It is the most profitable, because by

[117]Ecclus. 14:22.
[118]Ps. 103:24 (RSV = Ps. 104:24).
[119]Wisd. 7:14.

wisdom itself man is brought to the kingdom of immortality, for 'the desire of wisdom bringeth to the everlasting kingdom.'[120] And it is the most delightful because 'her conversation hath no bitterness, nor her company any tediousness, but joy and gladness.' "[121]

It has been suggested in an earlier chapter that St. Thomas was fitted by nature, by birth and environment, to achieve the metaphysical synthesis of which the world stood, and stands, in need. The blood of North and South alike was in his veins; the blood of poets and of men of imperial affairs. Humanism and philosophy, East and West, at Naples; contemplation, the sense of God, at Monte Cassino; philosophy and theology, and, again, the meeting of Eastern and Western thought, at Paris — these were the materials of his education.

"More than any other Western thinker, medieval or modern, he possessed the tranquil lucidity and the gift of abstract intelligence that mark the Hellenic mind."[122] The encyclopedic learning and the scientific zest of Albert the Great were put at his disposal. The

[120]Wisd. 6:21.
[121]Wisd. 8:16.
[122]Dawson, *Medieval Religion*, 76.

heritage of East and West alike was sifted in his mind.
The result was not a patchwork, an eclecticism; it was
a new thing. But in that new thing, in the organic unity
of Thomism, Thomas achieved a synthesis of East and
West as, in his blood, there was the synthesis of North
and South.

One of the most Western of Western ideas is the commercial evaluation of thought — the idea that thought
is one of the sidelines of life, one of many possible activi-
ties, useful for the results it can achieve in material ways.
The roots of this point of view can be traced back to Descartes,[123] and beyond him to the decadent Scholastics who
materialized what their predecessors had had to say on the
problem of knowledge and the nature of thought. From
the idea of thought on the one hand and of reality on the
other as the two terms of an opposition, it was a short
step to the question: "Is there a reality beyond thought?"
And as, from the nature of the premises as they were
then put, it was necessary to reply either, "No," or else,
"Yes, but we cannot know it," the pragmatist reaction
was inevitable.

[123]René Descartes (1596-1650), philosopher and scientist.

In either case, the unity of life is split. On the one hand, thought is the only reality; on the other, the material world is the only reality, and thought is a useful fiction insofar as it can be put to the service of action.

For St. Thomas, such a split is unthinkable. Thought and reality are not set in opposition, for indeed thought is reality. The actually intelligible and the actually knowing are one. Knowledge is a form of life; it is a process of becoming, of becoming more alive, and of becoming more alive because becoming other things: as Aristotle had said, the soul becomes in a manner all things.

Thus, "contrary to the popular idea of today, which regards the intellectual process as an 'epiphenomenon' on the surface of true 'life,' St. Thomas looks upon it as the life-process par excellence, and sees in it the deepest and most intense activity of intellectual beings. In opposition to those who see in intellect something necessarily egocentric, he makes of it the faculty which emancipates men from mere subjectivity; it may aptly be called 'the faculty of otherness,' if we may employ the term. In a wider sense, it is for him, as has been well said, the 'faculty of being,' the faculty which most truly grasps, and attains, and holds being. It unites in the highest degree subjective intensity and objective extension, because, if it grasps reality, it does so by becoming reality in a certain manner: and in that precisely consists its nature."[124] Thus, as Jolivet has shown, Thomism is idealist-realist. The realm of intelligible and intellect are coterminous. The world of extramental reality is intelligible; the world of intellect is real, and the highest form of reality, of life.

Wisdom, then, is the end of life in the sense that it is the highest form of life; and wisdom means primarily the becoming, through knowledge, of what is greatest and best, God, in the possession of whom all other knowledge and love will be unified and transfigured.

But this is to assume a great deal and to imply a multiplicity of problems. Is there a God? If so, can we know Him? If so, how? And in what way does His existence and our knowledge of Him affect the existence and our knowledge of other things? What is the explanation of human life, and of the universe as a whole? Can there be any certain answer to these questions? And if so, in what way will the answers affect the ordinary everyday affairs of life? In what way, especially, will the answers affect our

[124]Rousselot, *The Intellectualism of St. Thomas Aquinas*, 20.

evaluation of this sublunary world, and the things we most value in it? There is ineradicably fixed in human nature a desire for life, and more life, and ever more abundantly: can this desire be fulfilled?

St. Thomas, as we have seen, was presented with a number of very different answers to these questions. He was presented with a number of different approaches to the questions. He set out to answer them for himself; he set out to provide an explanation of the whole universe of being.

That explanation was to be a metaphysical explanation. He was not concerned, for example, with the biological investigation of man or the botanical investigation of plants. He had no desire to be a doctor, or a chemist, or an economist. He was concerned to discover and explain the place of man and plants, of medicine and chemistry and economics, in the scheme of life as a whole — to discover and exhibit their metaphysical significance. For without that metaphysical explanation, scientific knowledge is of relatively little use.

The first thing to note, then, is that Thomism is bound to no particular scientific theory. St. Thomas himself is at pains to point this out: he uses the theories current in his day by way of illustration, but with the proviso that these theories may well be discarded by a later generation and that such a discarding would have no effect upon his thesis. *Sapientis est ordinare*, as he quotes from Aristotle: it is the office of the wise man, the philosopher, to direct, to put things in order and, through his contemplation of the "highest causes," to provide the ultimate why and whither in the light of which we may make orderly use of science with its knowledge of the how.

Now, the initial problem with which Thomas had to deal was the problem, so hotly debated through the Middle Ages, of the way in which man can arrive at a knowledge of those highest causes that are at once the ultimate end of life and the directive of all other and secondary ends. "There is therefore," he says in the prologue to the fourth book of the *Summa Contra Gentiles*, "a threefold knowledge which man can have of divine things. First, there is that knowledge whereby he rises by the light of natural reason from the knowledge of created things to knowledge of God. Secondly, there is the knowledge given by the divine truth, which exceeds the power of human mind, coming down, through revelation, to our level, not as a thing evident because demonstrated, but as a word spoken calling for belief. Thirdly, there is the knowledge which is attained when the human mind is raised to the perfect intuition of the things that were revealed."

But what is the relation between these three types of knowledge? Is reason nugatory in view of Divine Revelation? Or will the findings of reason run counter to Divine Revelation? Or is reason to be regarded simply as the handmaid of theology, with no other purpose than to discover arguments in favor of faith and in disproof of those who impugn the things of faith?

St. Thomas begins by repudiating this last suggestion. "It is clear," writes Gilson, "how inaccurate it would be to interpret the achievement of St. Thomas in terms of a vast essay in apologetics; apologetics, with him, is only on the second plane, the result of a previous philosophic elaboration."[125] He had given himself to the service of truth, but he was rationally convinced of the ability of reason to attain truth within limits. Nothing, therefore, would induce him to tamper with the autonomy of reason in its own sphere. But was that to lead him to adopt

[125]Étienne Gilson, *Études de Philosophie Médiévale* (London: Oxford University Press, 1923), 122.

the pitiable expedient of the two truths? Obviously not. He could not conceivably accept this in its crude and literal form; but neither could he accept it in the form in which Averroists had held it: a combination of fideism in theology and skepticism in philosophy. Truth is one. The mind of man can know truth by its own natural light; the mind of man can know truth since God has revealed it; but these two testimonies cannot be contradictory.

"In the eyes of St. Thomas . . . it is perfectly meaningless to suppose that truths, no matter to what order of reality they belong, can clash with rational evidence. How could faith contradict reason? Faith, on the contrary, presupposes reason and perfects it. Antinomies can never be more than apparent: their hidden defect is always susceptible to the scrutiny of logic. Undoubtedly God has power to accomplish things that surpass the comprehension of man, but things that run directly counter to what is certainly perceived by the human mind God cannot do. Otherwise we should have to admit that God could contradict Himself. If, therefore, it is reasonable to accept a supernatural revelation with greater conviction than even the evidence of demonstration, that cannot be because it is anti-intellectual, but because it is more intellectual and endowed with a greater degree of truth."[126]

Other sciences, as St. Thomas himself says, have their certitude from the light of human reason, ratiocination; and ratiocination can be at fault; whereas the sacred science obtains its certitude from the science of God, which cannot be deceived.[127] Revelation thus can exercise a form of extrinsic guidance on the work of reason as such. As de Wulf puts it, "The prohibitive attitude adopted towards philosophical conclusions threatening or contradicting a dogma is merely a particular case of the general law of logical solidarity."[128] But into the speculations of reason in themselves faith does not penetrate; philosophy remains philosophy, its only criterion being objective evidence, its only light the light of natural reason.

To this autonomy St. Thomas will not do violence. If, for example, he finds no rational grounds for holding the noneternity of the world, he says so. And in general, the domains of faith and reason are clearly and categorically marked off: there is no attempt, as there was on the part

---

[126]Rousselot, *The Intellectualism of St. Thomas Aquinas*, 72.
[127]*Summa Theologica*, I, Q. 1, art. 5.
[128]De Wulf, *History of Medieval Philosophy*, 30.

of so many of his contemporaries or predecessors, to theologize in philosophy or to philosophize in theology. Thomas insists quite simply that there is a place for philosophy and a place for theology; and that in philosophy one should philosophize, in theology, theologize. The *Summa Contra Gentiles* is the perfect example. There are some things, Thomas says, that the human mind unaided can discover about God and about the world in general, things that "the philosophers have demonstratively proved, led by the light of natural reason." And it is that path that he follows in the first three books: the existence of God; His eternity, simplicity, and perfections; and His knowledge and willing. Then His power, His relation to creatures; creation itself, the eternity or otherwise of the world; the distinction of things, the nature of spirit, of man, of intellect. Third, good and evil, the end of things, the end of man in particular, the Providence of God, the divine law, the necessity of the supernatural (grace).

These considerations — of God Himself, of the coming forth of creatures from Him, and of the return of creatures to Him — having been carried through so far as human reason allows, there follows a fourth book. And it begins with a quotation from the book of Job: "Lo, these things are said, in part, of His ways; and seeing we have heard scarce a little drop of His word, who shall be able to behold the thunder of His greatness?"[129] What preceded had been of divine things insofar as reason could discover them; what follows is concerned with those things that have been divinely revealed; and here the truths that are to be found in the Scriptures will be taken as principles from which conclusions may be drawn, the criterion being always now the authority of Scripture and not of the human mind.

But, St. Thomas continues, what does remain to be proved is this: that these things, although suprarational, are not contrarational. This latter point is of extreme importance. No one marked off more clearly and rigidly than St. Thomas the respective domains of theology and philosophy. It was because he was quite clear as to what precisely differentiates them. It is not that their subject matter is altogether different. Both treat of God. They are distinguished, not by their subject matter, but by the light in which that subject matter is viewed. In one, the

[129]Job 26:14.

principles are given by faith; in the other, discovered
by reason. The content of what is given or discovered
may be the same.

And thus no one goes further than St. Thomas in
the interpenetration of the two sciences. For the unlet-
tered, the existence of God is an article of Faith, but it
can be proved by reason. And where reason has to acknowledge its limitations, where it comes to a mystery
it cannot penetrate or prove, still its work continues, for
the solidarity of truth must be examined and, negatively,
demonstrated. Otherwise there will not be a synthesis, a
unity.

It is an explanation of the universe of being that
Thomas sets out to achieve; and just as the whole of
reality, in its metaphysical aspect, is his subject matter,
so every means of apprehending truth is utilized. This
explains the apparent mixture of faith and reason in the
Summa Theologica. St. Thomas's purpose there is simply
to give as briefly as possible his world view, the complete
picture, as it is revealed in its fullness by reason working
on the data of faith reinforced by the data of reason.
Between the modes of knowledge, there is continuity
as well as solidarity. It is possible, from the materials

provided by the *Summa*, to work out a scheme of things on those lines. It is possible to build up a philosophy to the limits of the power of the mind, ending with the argument that to look for a divine revelation is reasonable if the natural desire of the mind to know God immediately is not to be vain. From there it is possible to go on to describe the new horizons in fact revealed in God's word — and their continuity with the boundaries of reason on the one hand, and, on the other, their own essential incompleteness — as being the boundaries of the realm in which truth is seen only as in a glass darkly,[130] so that they in their turn look further, to the realm of mystical knowledge, where the Godhead is still not seen indeed, but is sensed in the darkness of the cloud of unknowing. Finally, the point would be described at which that mystical knowledge reaches its fullness and prepares the way — beginning, as completely as the human spirit still on earth can do, the beatitude of Heaven — for that perfect vision of and union with the Godhead, in which all knowledge is included and completed and all desires are fulfilled.

[130]Cf. 1 Cor. 13:12.

To this ascending scale of knowledge, showing as it does how inaccurate it would be to describe St. Thomas simply as an Aristotelian with a pinch of Platonism, or, for that matter, as a Christian theologian with scattered pieces of Aristotelianism, we shall return later.

For the moment, let us follow St. Thomas briefly through the territory traversed by the sustained thought of the *Summa*. The view will inevitably be a superficial one, but it should give us at once an idea of the size of the territory and of its unity — of its size, for there is nothing that can pertain to the metaphysical plane that is omitted, from the almost non-being, the sheer potentiality of "bare matter," to the unlimited being, the absolute being, of the Godhead; of its unity, for this vast structure of treatises, questions, and articles is one organic whole, its multitudinous parts leading one to the other in a long logical chain, a chain indeed that describes the perfect movement, the circle, since it demonstrates how "all things return, as to their end, to that from which in the beginning they sprang as from a principle."[131]

[131]*Comment. in I Senten.* dist. 14, Q. 2, art. 2.

That is why, aesthetically, before we begin to investigate its claims to truth, to validity, we are bound to confess the *Summa* a perfect thing. There are no rags and tatters. There are no loose ends. There are no blind alleys from which no issue is possible. There are no exaggerations or overemphases, either in what is said or in the manner of the saying.

There is indeed a danger that the very simplicity of style of the *Summa* may mask its profundity. Father Joseph Kleutgen, S.J., writing of the theological depth of St. Thomas's thought as manifested in the *Summa*, says, "What makes this quality all the more remarkable, and what precisely hides it from the eyes of many, is that profundity of thought is allied in St. Thomas with a perfect simplicity and brevity of exposition. A superficial reading will not discover the profundity of the thought: a prolonged study is necessary. When, on a question to which St. Thomas replies in a few short phrases, one has followed the important researches of his commentators, and reflected long over the matter oneself, and then returned to the text of the saint from which one began, then, but only then, one discovers what a treasure of thought is hidden under the quiet covering of his few words. One is astonished to find already contained in them in germ what one had thought to have learned from others or from one's own reflections; and one recognizes that it was he who had led one through the paths that one had thought to be pursuing alone. His phrases, read over again, dissipate the difficulties which remain, and quickly marshal into a whole, a unity, the diverse ideas that have engaged the mind."[132]

That simplicity is adopted of set purpose in the writing of the *Summa*. The short prologue to the whole work is important. "Because," St. Thomas writes, "the master of Catholic truth ought not only to teach the proficient, but also to instruct beginners, according to the Apostle: 'As unto little ones in Christ I gave you milk to drink, not meat,'[133] we purpose in this book to treat of whatever belongs to the Christian religion in such a way as may tend to the instruction of beginners. We have considered that students in this science have not seldom been hampered by what they have found written by other authors, partly

[132]Quoted in M. Grabmann, *La Somme Théologique de St. Thomas d'Aquin* (Paris: Desclee de Brouwer, 1930), 136.
[133]1 Cor. 3:1-2.

on account of the multiplication of useless questions, articles, and arguments; partly also because those things that are needful for them to know were not taught according to the order of the subject matter, but according as the plan of the book might require, or the occasion of the argument offer; partly, too, because frequent repetition brought weariness and confusion to the minds of the readers. Endeavoring to avoid these and other like faults, we shall try, by God's help, to set forth whatever is included in this sacred science as briefly and clearly as the matter itself may allow."

"Whatever belongs to the Christian religion": St. Thomas, as Fr. D'Arcy has remarked, is "probably unrivalled in the size of his canvas."[134] It is not only dogmatic and moral theology in the narrower sense of the terms that he sets out to study in their biblical and patristic sources and in their applications; it is not only canon law, Liturgy, symbolism, and mysticism that he includes: the canvas comprises, and synthesizes, the whole of metaphysical thought, natural and supernatural, the realm of philosophy as well as of theology. But the whole is studied in this

[134]M. C. D'Arcy, ed., *Thomas Aquinas: Selected Writings* (New York: E. P. Dutton and Company Inc., 1939), x.

case from the point of view of the theologian, precisely because, in St. Thomas's view, philosophy and the "profane sciences" in general belong to the Christian religion.

But this vast ground is to be covered in such a way as to help the beginners; and it is this search for brevity and simplicity that dictates the order of the work so as to avoid not only all useless material, but also all repetition and all obscurity. The simplicity of structure of the *Summa* is strikingly revealed by comparison with the similar works of his contemporaries. Unlike the *Summa Contra Gentiles*, it follows the scholastic method of setting forth arguments pro and con, but here again it achieves a new simplicity and cogency.

The *Summa* is divided into three parts, the second part being subdivided into two. Each of these main parts is divided into questions; each question into articles. (This itself is a simplification from the abundance of divisions and subdivisions that was then common.) Each article has a title in the form of a question and begins with a number of arguments (and, again, in the *Summa*, it is a small number, avoiding "useless arguments") against the position that St. Thomas will adopt. Then, instead of an equal array of arguments for his position, there is a simple *sed contra* ("on the contrary") — a single argument, not usually of directly demonstrative value, being indeed often a quotation from authority, but pointing the way to the final conclusion. This conclusion is clearly argued and set forth in the body of the article. It is here that the position to be adopted is demonstrated; and this concentration of argument into a single body is what more than anything else gives the work its brevity, simplicity, and strength.

In his argumentation, St. Thomas is careful to distinguish between what can only be regarded as a probability and what is, to his mind, demonstrably certain. Moreover, the arguments and conclusions are strictly linked together; it is always to fundamental principles and certainties that St. Thomas returns, and the logical structure of the work permits him to refer constantly back to what has already been established.

After the body of the article, there follow the replies to the arguments with which the article begins, and in these St. Thomas finds opportunity either for throwing additional light on the main thesis and examining it from a different angle, or else of weighing the positions adopted by other thinkers, ancient and modern. (Often, of course,

this criticism is undertaken in the body.) And what is remarkable here is, on the one hand, St. Thomas's extreme
independence, which will not be intimidated by human
authority, however exalted; and, on the other hand, his
extraordinary capacity for finding valuable suggestions
and directives in the thought of others even though their
conclusions are in his view invalid. It was a principle of
his that there could be no such thing as undiluted error,
and he is faithful to his principle in his courteous treatment of those with whom he disagrees.

It is characteristic of St. Thomas's attitude toward
truth that, having set out to write a work for beginners,
he should at the same time have produced a work that
those who have studied him most deeply declare to be
inexhaustible. "When one has studied, time and time
again, the *Summa Theologica* as a whole, when one has
penetrated to the depths the problems it raises, when one
has steeped oneself in the other works of St. Thomas and
taken the pains to study the writings and teachings of the
saint in the light of the works of other great Schoolmen;
further, when one has familiarized oneself with his earli-
est disciples and commentators; finally, when one has
examined the relations between Thomist thought and

the thought of today; in a word, when one has made the *Summa* the center of a lifetime of intense intellectual labor, then, above all, one reads and studies this work without ever tiring of it; one takes it up again with a pleasure and a profit that are always new; and one can say with the classic commentator of the *Contra Gentiles*, the Dominican Master General Franciscus Sylvestris of Ferrara, who spoke of what he had himself experienced: 'Never have I had recourse to Thomas Aquinas without coming away the wiser, and the more devoted to him.' "[135]

It is the chief aim of theology, says St. Thomas, "to teach the knowledge of God, not only as He is in Himself, but also as the beginning of things and their last end, and especially the beginning and last end of rational creatures."[136] Hence the main divisions of the *Summa*. The first part discusses God in Himself and as the beginning of creatures. The second part discusses God as the last end of creatures and the way in which rational creatures return to God. The third part discusses Christ, who "as man, is our way to God."

[135]Grabmann, *La Somme Théologique de St. Thomas d'Aquin*, 135-136.
[136]*Summa Theologica*, I, Q. 2, prologue.

The first part itself falls into three main parts: the existence and nature of God; the Trinity; and creation. The first thing to be asked is whether there is a God, and this question St. Thomas answers by the famous five proofs. He dismisses the argument of St. Anselm, which was to be taken up again later by Descartes, as invalid, because of its fatal jump from the logical to the real order. His own arguments are based from the beginning on reality, on experience. He is later to argue the case for the real existence of the external world against skepticism, although in his day there was no need to give the problem the importance it later acquired. Having begun from the real, he can conclude to the real; and his conclusion establishes the existence, not, of course, of God as made known in Christian Revelation, but simply of the First Unmoved Mover who is, in Aristotelian terminology, pure actuality. That is all that the arguments prove, and it is all that they are meant to prove.

But it is possible to go on from there and to establish certain attributes of deity from the implications of the idea of pure actuality. This St. Thomas proceeds to do: His simplicity, perfection, goodness, infinity, immutability, eternity, and unity; His knowledge, will, love and mercy and justice — these are in turn discussed, and there is opportunity for the insertion of an examination of the nature of truth and goodness in themselves.

From divine knowledge and will, and the activity dependent on each taken separately, St. Thomas turns to the divine activity that is the outcome of both and deals with the problems of Providence and predestination. His answer to these — and, of course, all the preceding problems are logically linked together and interdependent — brings him to a point at which he might begin the discussion of the coming of creatures from God. But the *Summa* is a philosophical-theological world view — treating of creatures as dependent, not on the Author of nature simply, but on the Author of nature and grace. There is the mystery of the Trinity to be considered, therefore: the inner life of the Godhead as revealed to faith. With extraordinary profundity, St. Thomas brings reason to bear upon the data of Revelation: in what way we are to conceive of the "processions" of the Persons; of the Persons themselves,[137] their inner life; and, finally, their activity

---

[137]It is easy to misunderstand St. Thomas's treatment of the mystery of the Trinity; to regard his use of the Aristotelian category of "relation" as a brilliant *tour de*

in the world of creatures, the missions of the Son and Holy Spirit, and the indwelling of the Trinity in the soul redeemed. With the conclusion of this last question, St. Thomas has two modes of divine incidence into the world to consider, the natural and the supernatural; and he will return to them both later on.

He now turns to the "procession of creatures" from their eternal principle, and again his treatment falls into three parts.

First, he discusses the procession of creatures in itself: the idea of God as the First Cause, the problem of creation, the problem of movement, and the problem of multiplicity. Then, the problem of the distinction of things in particular: the presence of good and evil; the nature and cause of evil; the hierarchy of creatures — pure spirit, pure animal, and man, who is both spirit and animal.

> *force* that nevertheless does violence to the Godhead and empties It of infinity and mystery. St. Thomas is here dealing primarily with the nature of triunity itself insofar as the human mind can consider it; and his teaching must be seen in the light of the doctrine of analogy and also of what he has to say of the Godhead in Itself and of the agnosticism — "the most we can know is that we know nothing" — with which his whole effort at understanding concludes.

In the treatise on pure spirits, St. Thomas is enabled
to go deep into the question of the nature of knowledge
as such; when dealing with man in particular, he is at
pains to stress the fact that man is a psychophysical unity
and to elucidate the inferences to be drawn.

The third section of the treatise concerns the divine
governance of creatures — the way in which the divine
power is operative in the activity of creatures — and here
St. Thomas is at pains to stress the secondary causality
exercised by creatures, against the traditional teaching of
the Augustinians, and to explain how far this is from de-
tracting from the omnipotence or dignity of God; thence
he goes on to deal with the intermediate causality of spirits, both good and evil, in the world, the idea of fate, and,
finally, the power of one man to act upon other spirits or
upon material things, and the power of man as exercised
in the propagation of the species.

So far, then, St. Thomas has sketched a picture of God
and of the world as dependent on God. He now goes on to
the second part, in which the movement of man toward
God is primarily considered. The division of the second
part into two sections corresponds to the twofold consideration of this movement in its general aspects and in

particular. The first section, therefore, deals with the end
of man and with the types of means to be used in order to
achieve it.

Whatever end a man may pursue, whatever the "movement" concerned, it will be through action, activity of
some sort, spiritual or physical, immanent in himself or
external, that he will achieve it. Hence, the problem of
end once decided, the material with which the discussion
of means is concerned is human action from various
points of view.

In the first question, St. Thomas follows closely the
investigations of Aristotle in the *Nichomachean Ethics*.
He argues that all action is undertaken for the sake of
some end in view; that there is an ultimate end under
which all particular ends and desires are subsumed; and
he goes on to show, with Aristotle, that his ultimate
end cannot be riches or honors, fame, power, or pleasure.
Aristotle had been led to conclude that the ultimate end
must consist in the contemplation of the truth and in the
pleasure derived therein — leaving it unsettled which
was really ultimate, the contemplation or the pleasure.
In any case, his conclusion, to which his logic led him, is
not of a kind to commend itself to more than a very small

minority of men; and Aristotle was content to accept the fact.

But St. Thomas, while following the Aristotelian line of argument, carries it to a very different conclusion. He goes on to show that man cannot in fact be wholly happy in any created thing; that the contemplation of truth is in fact the contemplation, the vision, of the Truth; and that this vision, so far from being a cold cerebral activity, as Aristotle's conclusion suggests, is in fact a life of union with the supreme Beauty, the highest object of love, and that this life, moreover, is, in the phrase of Boethius, the whole fullness of an endless life together and the aggregate of all good things — an aggregate succinctly described in that prayer of St. Thomas which has already been quoted.[138]

The fact that such a beatitude is not impossible to man is next established and leads on to the next treatise, on human activity, the object of which is to discuss "what actions will lead us to beatitude and what actions will hinder us from it." In general and, so to say, at the deepest level, St. Thomas has already answered this further

[138]See pages 34-35.

question. For he has made a clear decision where Aristotle hesitated and could not decide: it is not subjective beatitude (pleasure) that is absolutely ultimate, but objective beatitude (union with God); the search for happiness in the sense of pleasure is subordinated to the search for perfection, the becoming like to God. The universe as a whole has as its end the reflection of the glory of God by the mirroring in its multiplicity of the beauty of the One, and this is achieved in the attainment by each thing of its own proper perfection, the perfection of its own nature.

In the case of man, perfection is reached through the actualization, in unity and hierarchy, of all the potentialities of his many-leveled life.[139] All minor perfections are subsumed under the first and principal, which is the possession by the spirit of the vision of God. In this life, in which man can attain an inchoate beatitude, perfection calls for as much knowledge and love of God as is possible. Now, because the perfection to be achieved in this case has God as its object and explanation — God the object of love and worship — because, in other words, a hedonist, self-centered union with God is a contradiction

[139]This is dealt with at more length in the *Summa Contra Gentiles*, Bk. 3.

in terms, it follows that not only is the selfishness inherent in pure eudaemonism avoided in the Thomist theory, but also that the essential orientation of life is already established in practice. It is an orientation that will radically affect the whole ethic that is to follow and make it essentially different from the Aristotelian ethic that, materially, it so resembles.

Moreover, it is here that St. Thomas solves the apparent antinomy between two radically different world views, between otherworldliness and humanism, between the Eastern concentration on total abandonment of self as the key to deification, and the Western emphasis on personal action and effort as the path to personal beatitude. The whole of what follows in this second part of the *Summa* is to be read in the light of this primary orientation: that everything, all human effort and all human desires and all human perfection, must be subordinated to the love and worship of God and to His power. The lesson will be reinforced, and the Aristotelian ethic again essentially changed, in the second section, in the particular discussion of the virtues.

The treatise on human acts opens with a discussion of human freedom: a profound analysis of volition, of all the elements that go to make a free human act, and of the factors that, on the other hand, rob the will of freedom. This leads to the consideration of morality: of what makes actions morally good or bad, right or wrong. And after the long and subtle treatise on the emotions, so valuable for its rich psychological insight, St. Thomas turns to the question of habits, those "dispositions" in mind or will that give us the capacity for acting well, swiftly and easily, and so are explicable in terms of acquired skill. They are also explicable in terms of a quasi-intuitive knowledge and, as such, are of immense importance for a right understanding of St. Thomas's complete psychology. The general discussion of habits, good and bad, leads on to the question of virtues: intellectual, moral, and theological; to an important section on the gifts of the Holy Spirit (where nonrational knowledge is again in point); and to an analysis of sin, actual and original, mortal and venial.

There follows the treatise on law. Here again St. Thomas achieves a synthesis, and therefore a transformation, of great importance. Before his time, there had been two different traditions: that of the jurists, working on the data of Roman law on the one hand and the Decretals of

Gratian[140] on the other; and that of the theologians,
comparing the Decretals with their own Augustinian
ideas of the eternal and natural laws. The result was a
considerable confusion. It was worse confounded by the
advent of a third line of thought: that of Aristotle. The
way in which all this conflicting material was utilized by
St. Thomas has been set forth by Dom Odon Lottin.[141]

The point that is of primary interest here, however, is
the way in which St. Thomas synthesizes the eudaemonist
and the legalist approach to morals, obviating the dangers alike of egocentricity and of voluntarism and phari-
saic externalism. This he does on two separate levels.
In the first place, he makes the natural law synonymous
with reason, its first principles intuitively apprehended
like the first speculative principles. The general laws of
human life thus become, not an arbitrary code dependent
simply on the will of God, but the pattern, dictated by

---

[140] A collection of thirty-eight hundred patristic texts,
conciliar decrees, and papal pronouncements covering
all areas of Church discipline, compiled by and including the commentary of the twelfth-century monk
Gratian.

[141] Odon Lottin, *Le Droit Naturel chez St. Thomas et ses
Prédécesseurs* (Bruges: Charles Beyaert, 1931).

the nature of man himself, of his own perfection. In the second place, he sets the Old Law over against the New as imperfect to perfect, and as what was written on tables of stone to what is inscribed in the heart of man; the substitution, in other words, of an internalized search for the true and the good, motivated by love, for the old way of external obedience to a code, motivated by fear — the spirit of freedom, in St. Paul's words, replacing the spirit of bondage.[142]

The law, then, both natural and divine, is not, and cannot rightly be viewed as, something apart from the search of the spirit for God Himself. The process of the Christian life to perfection is expressible in terms of the progress from obedience motivated by fear of sanctions to obedience motivated by love — obedience that ceases to be obedience in the ordinary sense of the term, since obedience presupposes a duality of will, and there is here an identification, the identification that is the essence of love.

The importance of this line of thought for the central question of activism and contemplation needs no

[142]Cf. Rom. 8:15. I have attempted to deal with this more fully in *Morals Makyth Man* (London: Longmans, Green and Company, 1938), chs. 5, 6.

121

stressing: the defection of the Western mind from the "universal metaphysical tradition" was due not least to the externalization of law and its divorce from its intellectualist basis.

The law instructs, but instruction of mind and heart is not enough. It has already been shown in the question on beatitude that man's final end is beyond his reach. He needs help, and help is provided by God's grace. There follows, therefore, the treatise on grace: its cause, nature, divisions, and effects. And with this, St. Thomas is ready to discuss the whole dynamism of grace, the life of the Christian virtues and gifts, in particular. This he does in the second section.

It would be impossible to follow his treatment in detail. What is of chief importance here is to notice the plan he adopts. His purpose throughout the *Summa* is to be as brief and clear as possible; and in consequence, he explains in his prologue that in order to avoid repetitions, it will be best to consider in one and the same treatise a virtue, the gift of the Holy Spirit that corresponds to it, the vices opposed to it, and the subsidiary virtues dependent upon it. This he proceeds to do, taking in turn the theological and the four cardinal virtues.

Now, in this latter consideration, he again follows the *Nichomachean Ethics* to a great extent, but the similarity is merely material, and there is a formal difference. This difference may escape notice precisely because of the form that the desire for brevity has given to the whole treatise. It will be found that the virtue of religion is considered, logically, under the virtue of justice. Nonetheless, it is religion that gives the whole its essential orientation. Eudaemonism postulates the acquisition of virtue, but pure eudaemonism is self-regarding. The Thomist ethic is theocentric; the whole life of virtue is "imperated by," subsumed under, religion, the worship of God; and thence again subsumed under the theological virtues, with charity at their head. In other words, the one thing necessary is the first consideration, and the moral life is seen only in function of religion and love, of self-loss in God.

This point is of such importance, being indeed the central point in the whole doctrine of man in his return to the eternal, that it may perhaps be insisted upon. A little later, when dealing with particular states of life, St. Thomas is to ask which is the better, the active or the contemplative; and his answer ultimately is that what is best of all is the life that is both active and contemplative, and in which action is the outcome and overflow of contemplation. The same idea is present in general terms in his treatment of the Christian life as such. There is the one thing necessary, the abandonment of self through love to God; there is also the life of action in general, and the activity that is the search for virtue in particular, and this must not be separated from the former, but, on the contrary, must be wholly subordinated to it, so that even the quest for sanctity is a selfless quest, a form of giving, the expression of love. It is this that the story of Bethany teaches.[143] It is this that St. Paul is affirming when he says, "You have not received the spirit of bondage again in fear, but the spirit of adoption of sons . . . and if sons, heirs also, heirs indeed of God, and co-heirs with Christ.[144]

If we think of goodness in terms of acting in accordance with God's law, then, St. Paul warns us, and St. Thomas after him, there are two very different attitudes we may adopt toward that law; and one of them, the one we are most inclined to adopt, is not the perfect Christian

---

[143]Luke 10:38-42.
[144]Rom. 8:15, 17.

attitude. He is speaking of Baptism, and he is explaining that Baptism is something very much more than an impressive ritual: it means that the baptized person is something wholly changed, something new; that the old relationship between creature and Creator, the relationship of servility, of fear, is superseded, and that in its place there comes the relationship whereby we cry, "Abba, Father."[145] The attitude we are tempted to adopt is an attitude of fear of the consequences that attend upon disobedience. That is the spirit of bondage. We need not consider it very long to see how poor a thing a life must be that is motived solely by this fear. There is a better, more dignified, more human attitude than that. The Ten Commandments are not arbitrary laws; they are not even specifically Christian laws: they are simply the signposts, discoverable by reason, to happiness. Better, then, to keep them, not from fear of consequences, but because they are seen as in fact the only creative way of living, the pattern of the perfect human life.

But this, in its turn, is not specifically Christian. This is pure eudaemonism. It is not what St. Paul means; it is

[145]Rom. 8:15.

not the spirit of adoption of sons. For here, too, the emphasis is on results; the attitude, in the last resort, is selfish. It is right so far as it goes: we have a right to want to be happy; we cannot want otherwise. But it does not go far enough. If self-regarding desire is the sole or the supreme motive of our lives, we shall in fact fail to find happiness; and we shall certainly fail to be Christians, because we shall fail to find the one thing necessary.

The whole of the law and the prophets, we are told by Christ, hangs upon the commandment of love.[146] Morality is a very shallow, and activist, affair unless it is subordinated to religion and to love.

We can find a parallel in the perennial story of the human heart. There comes to it, in the discovery of another personality, an overturning of the whole of life. The moment of vision that begets love changes the world, so that the old things are somehow different, and that universal change affects primarily ourselves. Life now means essentially a losing of self in another, and the discovery that things have meaning only as referred not, as formerly, to ourselves in isolation, but to ourselves as lost

[146]Cf. Matt. 22:37-40.

in and united to another. In losing our selfhood, in discovering that all our desires are summed up not primarily in our own good but in that of another, we find ourselves. For the true nature of life, as of love, is giving. The doing of the other's will becomes spontaneous, because there is in fact an identification of wills. "If you love me, keep my commandments"[147] might be truly expressed, "If you love me, you will keep my commandments, because your will is my will."

The modern Western world, because it tends to put the emphasis on doing, on practical achievement, on results, tends, where the life of the spirit is concerned, to put the emphasis on ethics, to make ethics the primary consideration. But what is primary is not the right way of doing, but the right way of being. In the Christian scheme of things, ethics is dependent on metaphysics in the sense that our doing will be right only if it is the outcome of our being. Moral virtue will be Christian moral virtue in its perfection only when it is the spontaneous expression of love, the giving of a personality that has learned the one thing necessary, learned the meaning of

[147]John 14:15.

religion and of charity, achieved the loss of selfhood in the discovery of God.

It is this central theme that gives the vast structure of the second part its unity and its grandeur; it is this that informs and transfigures the discussions of freedom and law, of virtues and vices, of grace and of the beatitude to which it is the means. It is this that enables one to see in the *Summa* the synthesis of the characteristic thought of East and West, and of the perennial problem of humanism and otherworldliness.

There remains the third part, for "since our Savior Jesus Christ showed us in His own Person the way of Truth which can lead us to the beatitude of life eternal, it is necessary, in order to complete the theological survey . . . to speak of the Savior and of the benefits brought by Him to the race of men." The treatise, accordingly, falls into two parts. The first considers the mystery of the Incarnation: the nature of the hypostatic union,[148] its effects, the reality of the human nature of Christ, its perfections and its defects (suffering, death), and the soteriological aspects of the Passion. The second deals

---

[148]That is, the substantial union of the divine and human natures in the person of Christ.

with the sacraments in general and in particular. And the whole *Summa* is brought to its conclusion by a consideration in detail of the life after death.

There are here two points of major importance that may be noted. In the first place, St. Thomas is determined to make clear the theandric character of the Christian calling. Christianity implies for the individual human being an ontological change — an ontological sharing in the divine nature — and this is effected through the person of Jesus Christ, true God and true man.

There had been heresies that, in their determination to safeguard the divinity of Christ, had reduced His humanity to a simple appearance and denied the hypostatic union of two natures in one Person. There had been other heresies that, to preserve the reality of the human nature in Christ, had whittled away His divinity. St. Thomas insists on the reality of both natures and on the reality of the union between them. Our Lord is true man: He breathes and walks and eats and drinks; He Suffers; He learns; He is tempted; He dies. At the same time, He is true God, and it is the divine Person in whom divine and human natures subsist, so that it is no metaphor, but sober truth, to say that God walked on earth, God suffered and died. And it is through the Redemption of mankind by the God-Man that man is called to a theandric life, to a real sharing, while remaining man, in the life of God.

From the need of that redemption, and that raising to a higher kind of life, no human being could be exempt, and so it is that St. Thomas, when speaking of the Mother of God, is determined to preserve that central principle — and the Church, so far from departing from him here, has canonized his doctrine. For the definition of the Immaculate Conception, while going beyond what St. Thomas actually stated with regard to the sinlessness of our Lady, was not least a defensive definition against those who, seeking to exalt the mother, would have taken from the Son, withdrawing a human creature from the universality of His redemptive work. It was just that universality that St. Thomas so unflinchingly defended, precisely because, if it was true at all, it must be true without exception. The redemptive work of Christ is the center of the Thomist theology of man.

A second point immediately follows. It has already been noted that the theology of the West tended to regard the life of grace predominantly from a moral point of view, in contradistinction to the more ontological

emphasis — the preoccupation with the deified life —
of the East. In St. Thomas, both aspects are present; the
third part links up with the second because it is through
the grace of the Redemption, brought to the spirit through
the sacraments, that the moral life is made possible. But
that moral life means, precisely, holiness: deification;
hence, the third part, so far from being a mere append-
age to the second, or, worse still, a treatise on the sacra-
mental system in isolation from the life of man, is in fact
the conclusion, the completion, of the second.

The *Summa* was never finished. St. Thomas was still
treating of the sacraments when he laid down his pen forever. The remaining part, now called the *Supplementum*,
was added after his death by Reginald of Piperno, who
adapted to the form of the *Summa* the corresponding
parts of Thomas's commentary on the *Sentences* of Peter
Lombard.[149] But although these pages from his early work
cannot make up for the loss of what he would have written in his maturity, the essentials are said, and the world
view is, in its main lines, complete.

[149] A collection by Peter Lombard (c. 1100-1160) of
expositions on Christian doctrine, taken from Church
Fathers, theologians, and scriptural tradition.

The second part is a metaphysic of morals, for it finds
its center in religion, metaphysical self-loss; and religion
finds its crown in that mystical union to which gifts and
virtues lead, and which is again the subject matter of
theology rather than of morals in any legal sense.

The last part of the *Summa* completes the picture,
because it leads us to the same conclusion from another
point of view. And this time the point of view is, in a
sense, the most comprehensive: the consideration of
the divine activity in the first part and the consideration of human activity in the second meet in the consideration of the theandric activity of the God made
man in the third; and from this we pass to the thought
of that eternal life of man with God in Heaven, which
all that has gone before is intended to prepare for and to
explain.

"The best interpreter of St. Thomas is St. Thomas,"
said Massoulié. The *Summa* is, as St. Thomas meant it
to be, succinct. It ceases to appear long-winded when one
has grasped the vastness of the territory covered and the
clarity with which, within that territory, the details stand
out in relation to the whole. From other writings of the
saint, there are precious commentaries and elucidations

to be obtained. Thus *Quaestiones Disputate De Potentia Dei* ("Disputed Questions on the Power of God"), *De Veritate* ("On Truth"), *De Spiritualibus Creaturis* ("On Spiritual Creatures") and *De Anima* ("On the Soul") throw added light on much that is debated in the first part; others, such as *De Malo* ("On Evil"), *De Virtutibus in Communi* ("On the Virtues in General"), and *De Caritate* ("On Charity"), are of help with the second part. The commentaries on the writings of Aristotle, in particular that on the *Metaphysics,* are an invaluable key to the Aristotelian elements in the Thomist synthesis. The early commentary on the *Sentences* of Peter Lombard, while sometimes of great interest as expressing a view that St. Thomas was later to change, often show the influence upon him of Augustine and Avicenna. The *Summa Contra Gentiles,* which was written as a textbook for missionaries among the Moors, is the book in which the relation of Thomism to Arab thought can best be studied. The *Opusculum in Boethium de Trinitate* ("Little Work on Boethius's 'On the Trinity' ") elucidates the nature of theology. The *De Substantiis Separatis* ("On Separate Substances") and *De Unitate Intellectus* ("On the Unity of the Intellect") enrich the psychology of the first part. *De*

Regimine Principum ("On the Government of Rulers")
gives more detailed expression to the political ideas in
the *Summa*. The scriptural commentaries throw light on
the biblical foundations of St. Thomas's thought; those
on Denys and Boethius, on his mystical doctrine; other
works — the *Compendium of Theology*, for example, and
the *Quodlibeta* — can be consulted with profit on many
points. Thus, the whole of St. Thomas's great output can
be grouped around his masterpiece and leads to a fuller
understanding of its teaching.[150]

At this point, it would be possible, and, for a complete
survey, necessary, to go back over the ground traversed by
St. Thomas in order to see where and to what extent he
used the materials he had to hand, and where he rejected
the conclusions of his predecessors — as, for example, in
the capital question of the plurality of forms in man, concerning which Peckham could say of the prevailing doctrine, "Hitherto the whole world had held it."[151] It would
be possible to investigate the metaphysic that lies at the
root of his thought, and that, through the principle of

[150]Cf. Grabmann, *La Somme Théologique de St. Thomas
d'Aquin*, 36-51.

[151]Cf. de Wulf, *History of Medieval Philosophy*, Vol. 2, 9-32.

actual and potential, brings every part of his philosophy and theology into the unity of an organic whole.[152] It would be possible to isolate the philosophy from his philosophical-theological synthesis and to show its validity and its coherence within the limits of its own territory.[153] These inquiries must be set aside here, in order to concentrate on the aspect of synthesis, and to note its significance for the present day.

As has already been said, philosophy and theology, having been rigidly distinguished from one another by St. Thomas, were far from being thereby left in a condition of humpty-dumpty irreparability. On the contrary, precisely because of the clarity and finality with which he had limited and distinguished their respective domains, St. Thomas was enabled to unite the two in a complete world view. But if we are to understand theology in the sense of a purely rational investigation of the principles of faith, and philosophy as a purely rational investigation of the data of experience, then the complete world view includes very much more than these.

[152]Cf. *Hastings Encyclopaedia of Religion and Ethics*, s.v. "Thomism."

[153]Cf. Gilson, *The Philosophy of St. Thomas Aquinas*.

In point of fact, it may be questioned whether we are right so to restrict the terms. St. Thomas has suffered for being interpreted in a rationalist sense. He was never a rationalist. From the nature of the case, his works present us with an investigation that is rational in method and approach. But in his whole theory of knowledge, of things human and of things divine, reason is far from being the only, or the most important, factor.

As philosophy, for all its autonomy, looks necessarily beyond itself — as indeed its whole achievement is to lead us to the point at which we are bound to look beyond its horizons — so the same is true of rational theology. It leads us far, but it leads us in its turn to a point at which we are bound to acknowledge that reason, even illumined by faith, can go no further. It ends in an assertion of ignorance. Negation, in the words of the Abbé Penido, is "the cornerstone of St. Thomas's teaching about God."[154] We come, at the end of all the researches of reason and faith, to the dark night and enter there "to unite ourselves in wise ignorance with Him who dwells in the shadows."

[154]*Le Rôle de l'Analogie en Théologie Dogmatique*, 109.

But it is not that the philosophical-theological synthesis breaks down. Within that synthesis, we are led further forward. As reason alone brings us to the threshold of faith, so the rational investigation of the things of faith brings us to the threshold of mysticism. And mystical knowledge has thus its organic part in the whole. Hence, the vital importance of those questions in the *Summa* that deal with the suprarational mode of knowledge in general, and with the intellectual gifts of the Holy Spirit in particular.

The place of intuition in the Thomist theory of knowledge, natural and supernatural, has not received the attention it deserves, and indeed has been obscured, because, no doubt, of the exclusive emphasis on reason and logic, the "Westernization," of the ages following upon the death of St. Thomas. Yet for St. Thomas himself there is no hesitation: not only is intuition in itself a higher form of knowledge altogether, implying as it does direct contact and union with the fully real, as opposed to the piecemeal perception that alone is possible to reason, but moreover, he is quite clear that just as it is in intuition that we find our last end, so it is from an intuitive moment that the work of reason itself begins, both in the speculative and in the practical orders. And it is, moreover, through moments at least of intuition or quasi-intuition that the poverty of reason is enriched and compensated for.

The illuminism of the Augustinians is rejected; there is no question of innate ideas; nonetheless the first principles, on which the whole ulterior work of reason is dependent, are themselves a "participated likeness of the divine uncreated light."[155]

Similarly, in the virtuous man, there is engendered a connaturality that enables him, without the necessity of reasoning, to judge intuitively what is to be done in this or that case. This point is of special importance in view of a legalist development that overtook the science of morals in the later Middle Ages, and which continued to color all but the first-rate thought of later times. The individual thing, if it is to be grasped in its wholeness, must be grasped intuitively; and similarly there must be an intuitive element in every judgment of a particular action as such before its goodness or badness can be decided.

It is here, as Père Sertillanges remarks, that St. Thomas "is very different from certain casuists. He considered it a

[155] *Summa Theologica*, I, Q. 84, art. 5.

contradiction to speak of really concrete cases of con-
science as solvable in the abstract, without reference to
the subject and circumstances of the particular actions. It
is impossible, he maintains, to define the individual by a
string of notions, and every moral case is essentially individual, and therefore 'ineffable.' This does not deny the
possibility of definite decisions in moral matters; it simply
maintains that this science has limitations and that facts
and conscience are beyond its scope."[156]

Similarly, reason must acknowledge its limitations where
the knowledge of God is concerned. "The intellect can
advance no further," says Maritain, "save as the disciple
of love." The four gifts that concern the mind — knowledge, understanding, wisdom, and counsel — are given
so that the obscurity essential to faith, which sees as in a
glass darkly, may be helped by the understanding of love.
There cannot here be full intuition of the Godhead; what
is possible is a direct, experiential, quasi-intuitive union:
suffering divine things, according to the pseudo-Denys.

In the first part, St. Thomas has noted the two ways in
which God is present in the world: as Creator, who, through

[156]Sertillanges, *Saint Thomas Aquinas and His Work*, 85.

His immensity, is everywhere, ruling the world without labor, enfolding it without sense of burden; and as the Author of grace, dwelling in the souls of the just. It is this latter presence that links up with the theology of the gifts.

The soul without grace is incapable of apprehending this presence. But the soul divinized by grace becomes "connaturalized," and capable not only of learning but also of suffering divine things. Through the gift of wisdom, therefore, the soul achieves a union with the Godhead hidden within it, whereby it judges of things as though with the eyes of God; and it does this because the union that springs from love has really made it one with God.

There is no need to stress the implications of this doctrine for a general estimate of St. Thomas's thought — to urge that Thomism is far from being the philosophy of Aristotle with an occasional pinch of Plato. "No philosopher," as Père Rousselot says, "has more intimately or vitally incorporated Platonism into his synthesis than St. Thomas."[157] For this is not an unimportant aside; it is at the very center of the Thomist synthesis. This quasi-intuitive apprehension of the Godhead is the link

[157]Rousselot, *The Intellectualism of St. Thomas Aquinas*, 36.

between rational knowledge and the ultimate vision:
there is a hierarchy, of Neoplatonist nuance, from
the humblest knowledge of sensibles, through rational
knowledge of divine things (philosophy), through rational investigation of faith (theology), through the suprarational knowledge of the gift of wisdom, to the ultimate
beatitude.

But the intuitive element in earthly knowledge is more
than a stage among many others. The human mind, St.
Thomas affirms, is always striving after intuition; and the
Thomist psychology, natural and mystical, might be described as an investigation of the nature and function
of reason, indeed, but also of the way in which, even in
this life, the limitations of reason are partially overcome.
Thus, the natural rational knowledge of things is enriched — and needs to be enriched — by the intuitive
grasp of the beautiful in the aesthetic vision, of persons
in the knowledge that is born of love;[158] and without this
intuitive element, life must necessarily remain cold and
arid, and the Thomist synthesis would itself be cold and
arid and, in this respect, no synthesis at all.

[158]For a discussion of this, see Thomas Gilby, O.P., *Poetic
Experience* (London: Sheed and Ward, 1934).

The same is true of the supernatural. But there is a further point of first importance to be stressed. It is this: St. Thomas does more than synthesize rational and intuitive knowledge in his whole view of the approach of the mind to reality. He synthesizes the knowledge, rational and intuitive, and therefore the love (for intuition here presupposes love), of created things into the knowledge, rational and intuitive, of the Uncreated. It is just here that the union of East and West, of otherworldliness and humanism, is ultimately achieved.

We have already seen that, for St. Thomas, the whole of life is to be expressed in terms of religion and charity — of that metaphysical loss of selfhood in God which is so far beyond any merely ethical quality of unselfishness. Morality has value ultimately as an expression of that metaphysical orientation of being, as a giving of what is demanded by the transcendent *Logos*, and as a giving whose motive is love. But the gift must be complete, and the imperfection inherent in all acosmist theories — all the negative ways of life that simply abandon created things, life on earth, and action in the world, as valueless — is precisely that they are limited in giving; they make restrictions in the name of a holocaust. St.

Thomas saw clearly that to love God is to love also the things that He has made. All truth is from the Holy Spirit, and, in the same way, everything good is from God and ought, if the offering of self is to be as complete a gift as possible, to be included in the gift. The lover's cry is always, "I wish I had more to give," and the spirit of man gives most when, being most alive, it has most to give.

Thus, the love and knowledge of created things, the love of science and learning, the love of nature and art, the love of men, the eudaemonist search for perfection and happiness, and the love of Christ even as Him from whom we have life more abundantly — all these things are not only compatible with, but are also demanded by, the fullest loss of self in the Godhead. The giving of self and everything else, which is the essence of Christian marriage, has its divine parallel.

This is again the key to St. Thomas's personalism, which is so far removed from the individualism of the modern West. The latter is characteristic of the shallowness of the rationalist-activist outlook, in which the accent is always on doing, and therefore on the doer. Thomist personalism is able to safeguard and indeed to emphasize the value and importance of the person, because it sees the perfection of the person as essentially centered in God and, derivatively, in other ends outside the self. The individual has a right to happiness and to the desire for happiness; the individual person is more important than the state; but the individual finds his happiness and perfection in the service of God and of society.

There is also a place for art; indeed, creativity is the natural right of every man, on whatever material or kind of material it may be his vocation to work. There is a place for that human love which finds its expression in procreation. There is a place for that passing on to others of the fruit of contemplation that is the intellectual parallel of the passing on of physical life, for all these things are in fact simply a giving of life to others in order ultimately to have more to give to the Other. The acosmism, and therefore the negation of life, so common in the mysticisms of the East, are thus avoided; so, equally, are the self-seeking, the individualism, the activism, and the commercialism of the West.

The originality of St. Thomas in all this is twofold. It consists, first, in the perfection with which he wove the endless threads of thought and of life into an organic unity, making these diverse interests not merely compatible but interdependent, and elaborating them into a hierarchy that leads every detail of the manifold back to the one; second, in the fact that he made sure, by keeping his thought free from physical theories and maintaining it always on the metaphysical, and therefore eternal, plane, that his synthesis would not be a dated system, would not be something static, final, and therefore bound to become obsolete. Thomism, as he left it, is "a vital organism, embryonic, but endowed with an infinite capacity for the assimilation of new truth and for adjustment to new conditions and environments without loss of its substantial identity. This precisely was his great gift to mankind: an ultimate synthesis, centered in God, so elemental and so elastic that it could include all future discovery and speculation, and, in so doing, both enrich itself and give unity to all human knowledge, past, present, and future. The tragedy of the subsequent history of Scholasticism and of European thought in general is its failure to have understood and utilized that gift to the full."[159]

[159]White, *Scholasticism*, 27.

Chapter Four

His way can heal the world

"God," says the old Spanish proverb, "writes straight with crooked lines." St. Thomas was destined not to be present at the Council of Lyons. He was destined not to convince his successors. His synthesis was destined to become the exclusive concern of a caste and to lose contact with the world.

Is his triumph yet to come?

If it is, then the centuries that have intervened since his death will certainly not have been in vain. That very cleavage between East and West which is so much to be deplored will not have been wholly without its benefits. We have gone our ways, yet the very fact that we have concentrated on our own isolated objectives may mean a richer total in the day of reunion. But when is the day of reunion likely to dawn?

There are signs that the message of St. Thomas was never more vital, never more needed, and never more

opportune than today. Two lines of thought suggest
themselves, by way of concluding this study.

The thought of the reunion of Christendom is today,
happily, in the forefront of the mind of the Church. It
is right and necessary that it should be, for never was it
more necessary that those who believe should be one
family and be strengthened by their unity to meet the
attacks — direct or indirect — of the forces of paganism
and disruption. That reunion will not come until there
is understanding of one another's points of view.

Now, between the Eastern churches on the one hand
and Rome on the other, that understanding does not yet
exist; and one of the reasons, if not the chief, would seem
to be the apparent incompatibility of the rational interpretation of Christian truth that is characteristic of post-
Renaissance Catholicism, and the intuitional, vitalist
interpretation characteristic of Eastern Orthodoxy. Dom
Clément Lialine speaks of the reaction of orthodoxy to
"the juridical and authoritarian," and "its predilection
for the vital and spontaneous," and quotes a remark of
Arseniev: "The word *authority* . . . applied to the super-
abundant torrent of grace which is the Church, sounds
almost a mockery." He notes the importance of studying

"integral knowledge, which is the heart of the message of slavophile philosophy, and which includes nonrational elements — intuition, affective knowledge, knowledge by connaturality, etc.," and adds, "The cognitive role of charity would here be studied, and might lead to an eirenic confrontation of Eastern and Western epistemologies." Thus Arseniev is quoted again as saying, "Many things remain obscure to us when we forget that the heart is the means and instrument of the most profound knowledge, and pin our faith solely to the investigations and researches of reason, as though 'only reason were capable of instructing us.' "

Again, Boratynskij writes:

Despising the heart, he has chosen for himself
Empty reason as his only guide.
So the heart of Nature is closed against him,
And the gift of contemplation lost to him.

"Russian poetry, philosophy, and psychology," says Vyscheslavzev, "are full of promise regarding the will of the starec to root reason in the heart. That is why Pascal, with his logic of the heart, is nearer to us than Descartes; and Boratynskij's correction of Descartes, *Amo ergo sum*

['I love, therefore I am'], is pertinent." Dom Lialine adds, "It should be emphasized that in all these quotations, which might easily be multiplied indefinitely, love is considered in effective relation to knowledge, and is not isolated in a dangerous sentimental vague: it is rather love-knowledge in fusion."[160] In conjunction with this should be taken another important fact: that "in the opinion of neo-Orthodox Russians, the principal task which confronts them is the construction of a Christian anthropology, preceding Christian thought having failed to accomplish it."[161]

Now, it is sufficiently clear that, just as there is much, not in the Catholic doctrine of the Church, but in the presentation of that doctrine by many modern Western Catholics, and in the emphases they put into their presentation,

---

[160]Dom Clément Lialine, *De la Méthode Irénique*, 62. It is, of course, always and only the mind that knows; the will cannot become a cognitive faculty. "Love," as St. Thomas says, "is said to discern insofar as it moves the mind to discern." And his great commentator, John of St. Thomas, explains that love can in fact alter the character of knowledge by passing into the very makeup of the object itself, so that there results an "affective experience"; but it is still the mind that, in the unity of this total personal experience, knows.

[161]Ibid., 53.

that cannot appeal to the sympathy of the East, so also there is much in the writings of post-Renaissance theologians that they will regard as wholly alien and antipathetic. But such cannot be the case with St. Thomas as he might, with perfect fidelity, be presented — and indeed as he ought, in fidelity to himself, to be presented in this case. For St. Thomas is the man suited to all occasions in this sense, too: that no one method of expressing his truth is necessarily more faithful to the spirit of Thomism than another, but that, on the contrary, Thomism itself demands that it be expressed in the idiom of the time and circumstances of those to whom it is addressed.

We have already seen that precisely those elements in knowledge that appear of most value to the Orthodox are given a place of similar importance in the Thomist hierarchy of knowledge. They do not bulk large in the *Summa*, because the *Summa* is primarily a textbook of rational theology for the use of Western students of the thirteenth century. It remains true that intuition, the knowledge in which the heart is necessarily involved, is for St. Thomas the summit of human knowledge.

It is the same, as has been seen also, with his moral theory, which is so far removed from the legalism that rebuffs the Eastern mind, and which, for that matter, has had so baneful an effect upon the Western. It is the same with his doctrine of grace, which is far more a matter of life, of dei-fication, than of moral action — the latter being second-ary and derivative. It is the same, finally, with his approach to law, where the external, the authoritarian, the legalist, is subordinated to the intrinsic, the spontaneous, the free.

Here, then, is a vast opportunity open to Thomism. It is not particular dogmatic differences that are of primary importance in the divided state of Christendom. The main difficulty is deeper: the apparent impossibility of ever be-ginning to think in like terms, of ever understanding one another's approach to revealed truth.

It is significant that, in this respect, Orthodox and Anglicans have more in common with one another than they have with Catholics, for Anglicanism has, of course, stood outside the post-Reformation tradition of Catholic thought, deliberately setting aside Scholasticism and going back to a consciously patristic approach to Christian doc-trine. Dom Lialine, noting that "Non-Catholics lay stress on the psychological differences in the Catholic Church in different epochs," quotes a remark of G. A. Glinz: "The question [of changes in Lutheranism] is reinforced

by the fact that post-Reformation Catholicism was not
by any means a direct continuation of pre-Reformation
Catholicism, but shows also new ecclesiastical formation,
the result of Ignatian-Jesuit mysticism"; and he adds, "F.
von Hügel, very sensitive to changes of this kind, chose
for his study on mysticism the pre-Tridentine figure of
St. Catherine of Genoa."[162]

Because, then, of the presence, and the importance, in
Thomism of those nonrational types of knowledge by which
the Orthodox set so much store, indeed it should be said
precisely because the evaluation given to them as against
rational knowledge is the same in both — there is obviously a great work to be done, a pressing need to be met,
by Thomism today. The same is true of the state, and the
needs, of the Western world in general, both in itself and
in its relation to the East, and therefore to the unity of
mankind.

[162]Lialine, *De la Méthode Irénique*. The words of the
French pastor A. N. Bertrand also deserve to be pon-
dered: "It might be said without paradox that what divided the Church in the sixteenth century was less a
question of theology than a problem in psychology."
And Dom Lialine's comment on them: "We shall see
that the apparent paradox in this sentence also applies
in Catholic-Orthodox relations."

The days of rationalist optimism are over, and we have witnessed in the twentieth century a reaction to reason in favor of intuition, emotion, and action. The systems of thought that had the most power in our modern world were Marxist Communism and that "energeticism" which found its extreme exponents among the Nazis.

Now, Communism is not antirationalist. On the contrary, it is a type of extreme rationalism, in which reason is exalted at the expense of every other approach to reality. At the same time, the essential of Marxism is its application of reason to an economic end as the ultimate criterion, and therefore its rejection of the Absolute. From its very nature, then, it seems that Marxism is doomed to disappear, for its nature is in direct opposition to the general tendency of our times.

Where Marxism is an anti-absolutist rationalism, the general tendency of our times is toward antirational absolutism. The flight to emotion, instinct, and so forth is accompanied by an insistence upon absolutes; and where a philosophy of instinct has set itself to destroy the worship of God, a pseudo-absolute is set up in the stead of God. It is this that gave the Nazi theory its strength. The days of individualism are over, as the days of rationalism are over.

Nazism seized upon the two leading characteristics of our time, and to that it owed its success as a philosophy.

It is clear that this view of life is indeed the lowest depth to which the West has ever sunk: it means, not only the impoverishment of life due to the abandonment of the supernatural, such as took place at the Renaissance; not only the further impoverishment due to the abandonment of all the suprarational forms of approach to reality, such as took place in the age of rationalism; not only the further impoverishment due to the restriction of reason to the domain of materialist science; not only the impoverishment due to the still further restriction of reason to the purely practical domain of materialist activism; it means, beyond all these, the final abandonment of the spirit altogether: the jettisoning of intuition and reason alike, of all contemplation. There is nothing left but blind instinct in the service of material ends.

That is why it is absurd to expect understanding between those who still hold to the way of reason, the idea that reason is meant to shape the order of international society through the building up of the structure of international law, which is reason's work, and those who have adopted the modern way of today — the rejection of the very postulates on which such a view of human society is based. It is idle to upbraid the upholders of this latter theory for their infidelity and their treachery, because there is no agreement as to the meaning of the words. Treachery to the one side means treachery to the law of reason; to the other side, the law of reason has no validity, and what is right is simply what instinct affirms to be conducive to success, success in its turn being measured simply in terms of power and force. From the international point of view, the deepest problem of our days is precisely this: these two opposing and contradictory versions of the very basis of human society confront one another; and there can be no possibility of a reconciliation between them as they stand.

What, then, is the position of Thomism here? At a superficial reading, one would be tempted to suppose that it must simply align itself with the forces of reason and against the forces of instinct. But perhaps it has something more constructive to do than that.

"If one considers the frightful spectacle which the nations today present," writes Maritain, "one is compelled to recognize this: that the spirit is humbled to the very depths of the earth. In truth, it is being punished for its own defections. It is the elemental forces of animal vitality which are taking their revenge against it, which are punishing it for having too long failed in its proper duties, failed human realities. There is no other resource left for the spirit but to go down, with the understanding of love, to the very depths of these elemental realities. Then, perhaps, later on, a new Christendom will be born."[163]

It is of little use merely to uphold the claims of reason against the new doctrines as one armed camp against another. Not by that way shall we save the world. On the contrary, there will be more and more defections from reason unless those who uphold reason can understand the cause of the defection, the crying need that lies behind the defection, the sense of frustration, of having been cheated, that prompts the rebellion; and unless, having understood that, they can first of all meet that need and remedy that sense of frustration.

And that rationalism cannot do. Something more than reason is required to remedy the effects of the bankruptcy of reason. For there are two very valid, if unformulated, desires behind the reaction to reason. There is first

[163]Jacques Maritain, "*La Liberté du Chrétien*," *Questions de Conscience* (Paris: Desclee de Brouwer, 1938), 219.

of all the desire for a better, more human life than the subhuman existence to which the age of rationalist optimism has led the mass of mankind. Implicit in this desire is the desire for a world view that shall break away from the shattering dichotomy of matter and spirit. If the East feels the need of an anthropology constructed, so to say, from above, from the plenitude of theology, the West can at least be said to feel the need of an anthropology constructed from below, from the tattered remnants of natural human instincts and intuitions of the good and the true. This anthropology would at least take account of the whole man and of the destiny of the whole man; take account of the value of personality, and of the need of the personality for a vital relationship to something other and greater than itself. It would remedy once and for all that evil division of things whereby philosophy pursued its calm and unreal course in complete lack of contact with the world of men and the sufferings of men, and an equally unreal, because equally abstract, economics forced men into servitude in the name of a progress that, on inspection, proved to be nothing more transcendent than the plump and prosperous plutocrat. Not on bread alone can man live, and if, in fact, the bread itself was

frequently enough denied, that was not the worst denial.
Most men wish to eat to live, and find it dull to have to
live in order to eat; there must be a *raison d'être*, an end,
a purpose.

Thus, the desire for a human instead of a subhuman
life is essentially connected with the second desire: that
which finds expression in the creation of the pseudo-
absolute, the deified state. Marxism will not admit the
worship of an absolute. Experience in Russia has shown
that the determination to worship will not be crushed
from the heart of man, and Marxism therefore, it seems
likely, was doomed. Nazism was in this at least far more
clever: it not only noted and made allowance for this desire; it adopted it and put it to its own service. Of course
there is an absolute, it said in effect; and of course there
must be worship, and mysticism, and love, the service of
the Other, and brotherhood. And in Nazism there are all
these things: state-worship, the force of instinct, the mysticism of race and blood, the selfless service of the collec-
tivity as expressed in the state. . . . It is no wonder this
gospel commanded such enthusiastic adherence and that
the youthful sectary found his life, in his faith, through
having lost it.

There is a basis of vital truth in all this, and the upholders of reason will find themselves more and more
diminished unless they take account of it. Man cannot
live on reason alone any more than he can live on bread
alone. The philosophy of Nazism was the *reductio ad ab-
surdum* of the defection of the West from the universal
metaphysical tradition; and if it can be seen as such, and
dealt with as such, it may be the remote beginning of the
return. At the moment, it was the ultimate extreme of
activism — an activism that is not only unintellectual
but anti-intellectual; not only valued above contemplation, but valued against contemplation and vowed to the
extinction of contemplation. But, paradoxically, it was to
the recognition of absolute values, parodied though they
are, that it inclined.

The greatest tension of our times is thus revealed as
the dilemma from the consideration of which we started.
In our day, it is the upholders of reason, if we except
Christianity, who jettisoned the worship of the Absolute; it is the opponents of reason and the upholders of
blind instinct who, under a different form, tend toward
it, although unconsciously and, alas, in so travestied a
fashion.

The West will not be saved by the triumph of one camp over the other. It will not be saved simply by the fusion of what is true in each and the exclusion of what is false. It will be saved only by the subsumption of what is true in both under the one thing necessary, in which the accent is once again put upon the dependency of the creature on the power of the Creator, the self-oblation in love of the creature to the Creator, and the need of making all action an emanation from and an expression of the contemplation by the creature of the Creator.

It is here, as has already been argued, that the West has much to learn from the East. But here again, as has also already been argued, there is need of more than the reception of a lesson or the accomplishment of a fusion. Maritain has remarked with deep insight, "This activism and pragmatism [of the West] are, so to say, the catastrophe of something which is very great indeed, but which the spirit of separation from God has jeopardized: the catastrophe of that generosity, that propensity to give and to communicate to others, that sense of ontological superabundance which comes from charity, and from holy contemplation overflowing into action. Whereas it has to be asked whether the impassible contemplation of the East, in which it sees its privilege, and which proceeds . . . not from the movement of descent of the uncreated Love, but from the movement of ascent of the energies of the soul struggling for a deliverance to be gained by force of an invented method and technique . . . does not, in its turn, betray, in the very spiritual order it-self, a sort of pragmatism incomparably more subtle, but which nonetheless shirks the witness which God expects of humanity."[164]

If we look for sanity and for fulfillment and happiness for our unhappy world, we shall find it, neither in action nor in contemplation alone, nor in a juxtaposition of the two, but only in that hierarchy of things which makes action the overflow of contemplation, and contemplation ultimately the gift of God — a gift that, in company with the action that it prompts, is given back to God with the giving of the self. It is just that inclusion of both things in unity and in hierarchy that one finds as the essence of the thought of St. Thomas.

But that means that a tremendous responsibility rests upon the Thomist. It has already been pointed out that

[164]Maritain, "*Action et Contemplation,*" *Questions de Con-science,* 153.

Thomism is no static, fixed system, but a living organism that not only is patient of, but indeed demands, constant renewal of expression; alteration, not of the essential, but of the accidental, of method and mode of presentation, of emphasis on this or that aspect according to the needs and preoccupations of this or that time and condition of the world. To be content to add nothing, in these accidentals, to Thomism is to be unfaithful to Thomism itself, because unless it is thus growing, it is not fully alive.

The primary need, in the context of method and mode of expression, for today is obvious. Whether we are thinking of the reunion of Eastern and Western Christendom, or of the present dilemma in the West, the first thing is to emphasize the dynamic and the intuitive-affective elements as opposed to the static and rational elements in Thomism.

This is perhaps especially clear in the case of law. It is the whole point of St. Thomas's teaching about law that there should be a passage from the "spirit of bondage" to the "spirit of adoption of sons":[165] that law should cease to be regarded as an external and even arbitrary imposition,

[165]Rom. 8:15.

and become recognized as simply the expression of the growth of the personality to holiness and to union with God. And this is true in degree of all law, which is made perfect insofar as it is internalized. In other words, its dynamic character is revealed. Once law comes to be regarded simply as an external fetish, the concept of law becomes inevitably static. Once it is regarded as simply the pattern of growth, and of a growth demanded by the nature of man or of the spirit, then it becomes dynamic. And the root of the present dilemma, insofar as it turns upon the nature and the existence of international law, is that its opponents regard it — not without some practical justification — as a purely static thing, and the enemy therefore of progress and change.

The same is true of morals; for morals, too, are a question of law, but with the same proviso: that perfection is to be found precisely in the internalization of its precepts, and that those precepts are, then, not a stunting of growth and of freedom, but the expression of the way to the full and final development of freedom.

In all this, then, it is the vitalism of Thomist thought, as of Christianity, that must be stressed; and for that reason, there is need of stressing the intuitive-affective elements in the theory of the approach of the mind, or rather of the whole personality, to reality. Thomism has suffered from too exclusively rational a presentation, although, as we have seen, it cannot in fact be adequately presented in purely rationalist terms. There have been times, of course, when it was necessary to stress the rational element; and, in a sense, that is still true today, but it can be done today only through a precedent emphasis on other things. We shall not win the world back to reason unless we can first show that by *reason* is not meant the impoverished reason of rationalism, but reason as one of the elements in a whole approach to reality — necessary but not the only thing necessary, important but not the only thing important.

It is the main criticism leveled by Eastern Christian thinkers against Christians of the West that by overstressing the role, and the competence, of reason, they have tended to diminish the mystery and the majesty of God revealed. We, on our side, have a right to a countercriticism: that in their very reaction to rational clarity and order, they have overlooked the fact that God expects of humanity an integral approach, in which philosophy, theology, and mysticism are all elements, and elements that cannot be left in ultimate contradiction without sinning against the unity of truth.

But criticism and countercriticism are not enough. It is for us on our side also to recognize the element of truth in the reproaches made by the East against us, to recognize the fact that there has been, in Western theology, and in post-Tridentine theology particularly, too exclusive an emphasis on the rational-theological approach. Second, it is for us to show that that overemphasis does not exist in the organic fullness of St. Thomas's doctrine. Finally, it is for us to make good our deficiencies by imitating his wholeness, in the hope that thus, by a common self-correction, West and East together may come to mutual understanding and to the common possession of the completeness of truth.

Insofar as there is in the non-Christian world at large a similar aspiration after an approach that is mystical or intuitive in character, even though it finds expression actually in a pseudo-mysticism, a similar duty confronts us. But here there is a further and greater difficulty to be met. It has been expressed very forcibly by Professor Mortimer J. Adler in his *St. Thomas and the Gentiles*. "Wherever in the secular universities," he writes, "there has been a revival of interest in medieval philosophy, leading inevitably to an enthusiasm for St. Thomas, it was not long before another renaissance occurred, a revival of the cries against Scholasticism, authoritarian dogmatism, the antiscientific spirit, metaphysical verbalism, an outmoded formal logic, and a puerile subservience to antiquity, especially the scheme of Aristotelian categories. We must not be allowed to forget that all the values most prized by modern men were won by a struggle against the decadent Scholasticism of the fifteenth and sixteenth centuries. The sudden threat of Thomism quite naturally awakens the passions which preceded the birth of modern times. If we are surprised at the vehemence with which the spirit of the Renaissance re-asserts itself to prevent any backsliding, it can only be because we had not understood our allegiance to St. Thomas as a signal for backsliding. In the name of St. Thomas we should be even more opposed than Francis Bacon, David Hume, and the rest to the corrupt Scholastics of the Renaissance, with their logic-chopping and their senseless opposition to the findings of scientific research. It is we, not St. Thomas, who have been misunderstood, and the fault is ours. . . . We have appeared as so many Don Quixotes proclaiming the beauty of Dulcinea del Toboso to a world that could only see an ugly hag being snatched from the grave. . . . We who have thought that we were bringing light from a source which the modern world had needlessly neglected are charged with obscurantism. Is it possible that we defeated our purpose by speaking the words of ages still generally regarded as dark? . . . In calling ourselves Thomists, we have thought only to declare our devotion to the cause of philosophy itself, to the truth which is above the partisan claims of divisive schools. But we find that we are regarded as belonging to a cult, to a movement dangerously subversive of the prevailing culture. Thomism is not the proper name for philosophy in its perennial vitality. It is just one 'ism' among many, and an anachronism at that."[166]

The belief in progress still lingers, more unconsciously now than consciously, no doubt, in our world; and it is largely responsible for the conviction that a philosophy, however brilliant, that is medieval cannot be valid or useful for the world of today. One of the first things we have to fight is this temporalization of what is by its nature

[166]Mortimer J. Adler, St. Thomas and the Gentiles (Milwaukee: Marquette University Press, 1938), 3-5, 7.

extratemporal. We have to agree indeed that the history
of the human spirit is, in one sense, a history of a progress,
and that it is far from being our intention to revert to the
Middle Ages and discard all the philosophical riches that
have been won since that time. But, on the other hand,
we have to urge that if the deepest springs of truth, in
which all secondary achievements must be integrated,
have indeed ever been plumbed at all, it is obscurantist
and perilous to allow considerations of date to influence
us in our estimate of where the truth regarding them lies.
But if, in our urging of our case, we in fact think and speak
in the idiom of a bygone age, then we must expect to be
misunderstood: it is we, also, who are temporalizing our
thought, although in a different way.

If we have a warning against that, in the unhappy
history of those Scholastics who, during the Renaissance,
continued to speak, and to think, in terms that had lost
their vitality for the contemporary world, and who refused
to face the problems that were of primary importance to
the contemporary world, we have also a positive example
in the person of St. Thomas himself. If we do in our day,
so far as we may, what he did in his, we shall be contrib-
uting as we ought to the growth of Thomism. His mind

was open to all contemporary questions and points of view; he studied the views of his adversaries with sympathy, and therefore understood them; he spoke in a language appropriate to his time; he believed with his whole heart that "everything that is true comes from the Holy Spirit"; he brought whatever he found of truth into the unity of his own synthesis.

We do not, like him, have to think out the essentials of that synthesis — which is fortunate, for we would be quite incapable of doing it. But we have to enlarge and enrich the synthesis with the findings of later and contemporary thought and to recast it in terms of contemporary thought. And because there is, as Professor Mortimer J. Adler has shown, that Renaissance antagonism at the root of the contemporary antagonism, it is not the least of our duties to show that just as during his life, there was no lack of understanding between the schools of arts and St. Thomas, so at the time of the Renaissance, there was no need for misunderstanding between the positive preoccupations of the humanists and St. Thomas. How could there be, since St. Thomas is par excellence — and par excellence because most consistently — the Christian humanist?

At the call of Leo XIII, Thomism emerged from the ecclesiastical schools to face the world again. It is significant that perhaps the best-known Thomist names are those of laymen: Gilson and Maritain in France, Adler in America. It is, at any rate, good to be able to say that whatever may be thought of the validity of their conclusions, there can be no disputing the fact that Thomists are indeed facing the problems that confront the world of today and dealing with them in an actual and modern manner.

This is especially the case in the country where Thomism recently flourished: France. Besides the work of deepening and widening our grasp of Thomism itself, the historical research to which Père Mandonnet gave so magnificent an impetus, and the invaluable work that is being done in such problems as that of reunion with Eastern and other dissident confessions, there is a magnificent promise for the future, as well as a considerable achievement in the present, in the diverse publications of the *éditions du cerf*, which explore in the light of Thomist principles the problems — political, sociological, and cultural — that weigh upon our world. Such work is sufficient to prove that, so far from being dead, Thomism was never more alive.

The Aquinas Prescription

The triumph of St. Thomas is yet to come. But triumph for him does not mean the routing of enemies, because his whole work, and his whole life, were simply the service of the Light; and that Light is the Life of men. It is platitudinous to say that all our needs could be summed up in the need for unity; we are split by economic divisions between classes, by political rivalries between nations, by ideological differences, and by the clash of supporters and opponents of reason, of supporters and opponents of faith. Above all, the life of our world is split into a thousand fragments because of our defection from metaphysics; the various levels of life cannot be unified because the one unifying factor has been excluded; and it will never be unified, and consequently the world will never be sane, until that metaphysical level is rediscovered and the manifold levels of life are re-integrated into its unity. It is unity above all that characterizes the wisdom of St. Thomas, for in him there was equally the wisdom of the humanist and the poet, the wisdom of the philosopher, the wisdom of the theologian, and the wisdom of the mystic; and all these were one.

It belongs to the wisdom that includes all other wisdoms, the wisdom that is the gift of the Holy Spirit, not only to contemplate divine things, but also to order human action.[167] And the best life is that in which contemplation of divine things does in fact overflow into action.[168] When that is the order of things — when action is the overflow of contemplation, and the expression, ultimately, of the total self-giving of love — then, from that unity of life, there follows order and that for which the whole world longs today: peace.

It is the office of the wise man to put things in order, and of the wise man in the deepest sense to put things in divine order. But peace is, in Augustine's phrase, the tranquillity of order, so, from wisdom, there follows peace. There is no easy way to real happiness and joy, but there is a sure way. It is the way of the discovery of the one thing necessary, the way of divine wisdom.

"Contemplation can be filled with joy in two senses. First . . . contemplation of the truth is proper to man by reason of his nature, for he is a rational animal, whence it is that 'all men by nature desire to know,' and so find joy in the contemplation of truth. And for him who has the

[167]*Summa Theologica*, II-II, Q. 45, art. 6.
[168]Ibid., Q. 188, art. 6.

habit of knowledge and wisdom the joy is the greater, since thereby contemplation is free of difficulty. But in another way, contemplation is made joyous on account of its object, that is to say, when a man contemplates something he loves. So bodily sight is a thing of joy, not only because seeing is in itself pleasant, but also because the faculty of sight enables one to see a person one loves. Therefore, since the contemplative life consists primarily in the contemplation of God, to which love moves us . . . it follows that in that life there is joy, not only because of the contemplation in itself, but also because of the divine love. And as to both, the joy exceeds any joy that is known to man, for the joy of the spirit is stronger than that of the flesh, as was shown above in treating of the emotions; and the love whereby God is loved in charity is greater than all other love. Whence it is said in Psalm 33: "Taste and see that the Lord is sweet."[169]

St. Thomas's first recorded question was "What is God?" and it was when he had found the answer with a fullness not given to most men that he spoke of his writings as straw. It was time for him to go — to find that joy

[169] *Summa Theologica*, Q. 180, art. 7.

of which it is written, in contrast with all other joy, "Enter thou into the joy of thy Lord."[170] To that joy, all the volumes of his works are an introduction. And it is because of that, because they are solely concerned to give testimony, not to Thomas, but to the Light, that one finds in them a reflection of the glory of the Light, and might apply to them, by that process of analogy of which St. Thomas himself made such fertile use, the words addressed by Augustine to the Light Itself: "O Beauty ever old and ever new."[171]

[170]Matt. 25:21.
[171]*Confessions*, Bk. 10, ch. 27.

Biographical Note

Gerald Vann
(1906-1963)

Born in England in 1906, Gerald Vann entered the Dominican Order in 1923 and, after completing his theological studies in Rome, was ordained a priest in 1929. On returning to England, he studied modern philosophy at Oxford and was then sent to Blackfriars School in Northhamptonshire to teach and later to serve as headmaster of the school and as superior of the community there. Tireless in his efforts to bolster the foundations of peace, he organized the international Union of Prayer for Peace during his tenure at Blackfriars.

Fr. Vann devoted his later years to writing, lecturing, and giving retreats in England and in the United States, including lecturing at Catholic University of America in Washington, D.C. He wrote numerous articles and books, many of them drawing on the wisdom of St. Thomas Aquinas, who influenced him greatly. Fr. Vann's writings combine the philosophy and theology of St. Thomas with the humanism emphasized in the 1920s and 1930s. His works reflect his keen understanding of man's relationship to God, his deep sensitivity to human values, and his compassionate understanding of man's problems and needs. Particularly relevant in today's divided world is his appeal for unity, charity, and brotherhood. His words reveal what it means today to fulfill the two greatest commandments: to love God and to love one's neighbor.

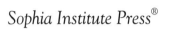

Sophia Institute Press®

Sophia Institute is a nonprofit institution that seeks to restore man's knowledge of eternal truth, including man's knowledge of his own nature, his relation to other persons, and his relation to God.

Sophia Institute Press® serves this end in numerous ways: it publishes translations of foreign works to make them accessible for the first time to English-speaking readers; it brings out-of-print books back into print; and it publishes important new books that fulfill the ideals of Sophia Institute. These books afford readers a rich source of the enduring wisdom of mankind.

Sophia Institute Press® makes these high-quality books available to the general public by using advanced technology and by soliciting donations to subsidize its general publishing costs.

Your generosity can help Sophia Institute Press® to provide the public with editions of works containing the enduring wisdom of the ages. Please send your tax-deductible contribution to the address below. We also welcome your questions, comments, and suggestions.

For your free catalog, call:
Toll-free: 1-800-888-9344

or write:
Sophia Institute Press®
Box 5284, Manchester, NH 03108

or visit our website:
www.sophiainstitute.com

Sophia Institute is a tax-exempt institution as defined by the Internal Revenue Code, Section 501(c)(3). Tax I.D. 22-2548708.